Common
Psychological
Disorders
in Young Children

Common Psychological Disorders in Young Children

A Handbook for Early Childhood Professionals

JENNA BILMES and TARA WELKER, PhD

Redleaf Press
www.redleafpress.org

Published by Redleaf Press
a division of Resources for Child Caring
10 Yorkton Court
St. Paul, MN 55117
Visit us online at www.redleafpress.org.

First edition 2006
Cover designed by Amy Kirkpatrick
Interior typeset in Janson Text and designed by Brian Donahue / bedesign, inc.
Printed in the United States of America
13 12 11 10 09 08 07 06   1 2 3 4 5 6 7 8

Redleaf Press books are available at a special discount when purchased in bulk for special premiums and sales promotions. For details, contact the sales manager at 800-423-8309.

Library of Congress Cataloging-in-Publication Data
Bilmes, Jenna, 1948-
  Common psychological disorders in young children : a handbook for early childhood professionals / by Jenna Bilmes and Tara Welker. — 1st ed.
      p. cm.
  Includes bibliographical references and index.
  ISBN-13: 978-1-929610-91-4 (alk. paper)
  ISBN-10: 1-929610-91-2 (alk. paper)
  1. Child psychopathology—Handbooks, manuals, etc. I. Welker, Tara. II. Title.
  RJ499.3.B55 2006
  618.92'89—dc22

                    2006014043

Printed on acid-free paper.

For my mom and dad.
—JENNA BILMES

For Dan and Mia. You make my world go 'round.
—TARA WELKER

CONTENTS

INTRODUCTION

Malia is a happy, friendly four-year-old. She can't wait to get in the door in the morning to greet her teacher and share some bit of news. Malia is "best friends" with Erin, and the two spend much of their free time in the art area making all kinds of creative projects of their own design. Malia loves group time, and often requests her favorite stories or songs. She is very familiar with the routines of the classroom and takes new children under her wing to guide them through the day. "When I grow up, I'm going to be an animal doctor and help all the sick horses," she says.

Rachel is in the same classroom as Malia. She often has an unkempt look when she arrives at school, and she is sometimes wearing the same clothing she went home in the day before. A serious child, Rachel often looks down, so as to avoid eye contact with others. While Malia and Erin are exploring the world, Rachel usually takes her baby doll from her cubby and sits by herself under the loft. She comes to group meetings when called, but never participates. Instead, she sucks on her thumb and rocks back and forth while others are singing or chatting about the story or activity everyone shared. Every day, providers have to remind her to wash before lunch and to put on her shoes after rest time. When asked if she would like more snack, what song she'd like to sing, or what activity she'd like to do, her common response is a very soft "I don't know."

Four-year-old Tommy's first day of school seemed very uneventful. He was quiet and observant, and very polite to adults. On the second day of school, the teachers found him under the loft, pulling the fins off the pet goldfish. A few days later, he soiled his pants at rest time. Teachers then began to report that he would eat nothing except fresh fruit or individually packaged crackers. At the beginning of the second week of school, a teacher found him with another young boy in the bathroom. He was trying to get the other child to engage in sex play. His custodian grandmother said he just needed time to get used to the new school.

I f you're like most teachers and providers, at times you've been concerned about some of the ongoing behaviors of children in your care. Maybe you have a child who seems very fearful and doesn't join group activities. Perhaps one of the children often hits or bites other children, or maybe a child won't stop picking up hairs off the floor. When children act in such unusual ways, you sense something isn't quite right. You may suspect mental illness, abuse, or neglect. In some cases, the family may have already told you that their child is on medication or is receiving some other treatment for a psychological disorder. Whether or not a child has been diagnosed with a mental illness, children with behavioral and mental health problems can leave you feeling frustrated and confused. You may be struggling to balance supporting the child with providing a safe, healthy, and challenging environment for all the children in your care.

In this book you will learn more about mental health, mental illness, and the specific psychological (also called psychiatric) disorders that affect children. You will also learn many practical classroom and child care setting strategies that will make it easier for you to help such children be successful in school and in life, as well as some ways to work with parents as partners in addressing these challenging issues.

Stereotypes about Mental Illness

Over the last fifty years or so, a lot of progress has been made in understanding the nature and causes of mental illness. Rather than seeing it as a personal flaw or the work of mysterious supernatural forces, behavioral and brain scientists have established that mental illness usually develops from a complex interaction of inborn, familial, cultural, and environmental influences.

And yet stereotypes and prejudices persist about people who have been diagnosed with a psychological disorder. Too often, people with mental illness are still labeled as "crazy," and are feared and even ostracized. Most troubling is that people sometimes ignore the symptoms of a psychological disorder in themselves or in a family member because of these misunderstandings. When this happens, the problems and suffering associated with the disorder go untreated until there's a crisis.

Mental Illness Is Common and Treatable

The truth is, these disorders are more common than most of us think. And with the progress that has been made in the understanding of brain chemistry, heredity, and human behavior, they are more treatable than ever.

Mental illness does not discriminate by age, gender, socioeconomic group, or education. An estimated 26.2 percent of Americans ages eighteen and older (or one in four adults) suffer from a diagnosable mental disorder in a given year (Kessler et al. 2005). It has been estimated that more than 6 million young people in America suffer from a mental health disorder that severely disrupts their ability to function at home, in school, or in their community (Surgeon General 1999).

Some mental disorders can be quickly and easily treated and managed. Others, while treatable, can produce severe lifelong impairment. For example, many people with depression can manage their disorder while continuing normal daily activities. They can be helped by such measures as lifestyle changes combined with support from family and friends, a few sessions with a counselor or minister, or a combination of medication and psychotherapy. Even people with more-debilitating mental illnesses, such as schizophrenia or bipolar disorder, can lead happy, productive lives with appropriate support and professional intervention.

Mental Illness in Children

Sometimes it's hard to tell whether or not a person's behavior is a disorder. Each of us has a unique personality, with individual ways of being and acting in the world. Things get trickier when we're talking about children, because children naturally develop and change very quickly over a relatively short period of time. What is normal for a *young* child may be a sign of trouble in an older child. For example, a temper tantrum in a two-year-old is not unusual, but a temper tantrum in a fifteen-year-old would cause concern. When we also take into account the unique inborn qualities and the early experiences of individual children—along with the influences of their family and other caregivers, their culture, and their environment—evaluating a child's behavior becomes even more challenging.

MENTAL HEALTH

in childhood and adolescence is defined by the achievement of expected developmental cognitive, social, and emotional milestones and by secure attachments, satisfying social relationships, and effective coping skills. Mentally healthy children and adolescents enjoy a positive quality of life; function well at home, in school, and in their communities; and are free of disabling symptoms of psychopathology (Hoagwood et al. 1996).

DEFINING MENTAL HEALTH AND ILLNESS IN CHILDREN

While defining mental health and mental illness in children is not easy, it's still important to have a working definition of these terms. The Surgeon General's report on children and mental health (U.S. Department of Health and Human Services 1999) defines mental illness in children as "serious deviations from expected cognitive, social, and emotional development." The phrase "serious deviations" contains several assumptions that are important to consider when thinking about mental illness. For example, is it a "serious deviation" if an unusual behavior happens only once or only at home? In order to be considered a disorder, the following must also be true:

- **The symptoms occur often and last a long time.** Different disorders have different frequency and duration criteria, but the general idea is that the symptoms are persistent over time and don't just happen on occasion.

- **The symptoms are present in more than one setting.** The child's symptoms must appear in more than one environment, such as home, school, religious settings, or other social environments.

- **The symptoms cause significant distress and/or impairment in functioning.** The child's symptoms must make it difficult for him to grow and develop as expected. Examples include: a child with attention problems who is not learning academically, a child who is withdrawn and not learning social skills, or a child who is aggressive and unable to follow basic school limits and expectations or who is unable to make friends.

MEETING THE CHALLENGE OF CHILDREN UNDER STRESS

In early childhood classrooms and child care settings across the United States, teachers and providers are reporting that children are showing more and more signs of stress, from being withdrawn to being out of control. Many teachers say they find it more challenging than ever to provide a safe and healthy environment for all the children in their care. Learning how to respond effectively to behavioral challenges and understanding the psychological disorders that underlie some of these behaviors can make it easier for teachers to meet this challenge.

About This Book

This book was written to help you answer questions about your role as an early childhood professional in dealing with behavioral and mental health issues that may arise with the children in your care.

In chapter 1, we talk about typical milestones and influences in the development of early childhood mental health. Chapter 2 helps steer your observation of children so you can be alert to possible emotional or behavioral challenges that might require further investigation. In chapter 3, you will learn how to introduce ongoing strategies into your program—strategies designed to support children with behaviors that put them at risk for developing social/emotional problems—and how to support children who have been formally diagnosed with mental illness. In chapter 4, we discuss the importance of developing mutually respectful relationships with families in order to best communicate and work together on strategies to support their child. Finally, the eight chapters in Part 2 of this book summarize common mental disorders found in young children, including typical behaviors, causes, treatments, and classroom and child care setting strategies.

The field of early childhood psychology is relatively new, and advances are being made all the time. New drugs, treatments, and diagnostic techniques are constantly being developed to help families and other caregivers understand and manage psychological disorders in the children in their care. As a provider and teacher in an early childhood setting, you are an important partner in that process, and you can help children with such disorders learn and thrive during one of the most critical times in their lives.

PART

1

Understanding and
Responding to
Psychological Disorders
in Young Children

We do what we know,
and when we know better,
we do better.
—MAYA ANGELOU

CHAPTER 1: Factors in the Development of Mental Health in Children

As we discussed in the introduction, the development of mental health in young children is the product of both nature and nurture. Each child enters the world with a unique set of factors that will influence how she develops. At the same time, there are many ways that a child's family, culture, and environment can shape and influence her development, behavior, and mental health.

Two children may be born with a similar tendency to develop a certain mental disorder, such as depression, perhaps because of a genetic predisposition. If one of these children develops a strong attachment to a nurturing parent and has a predictable, supportive environment, the chances decrease that he will develop that disorder. If the other child is passed from one foster home to another and experiences life as a series of dangerous and unpredictable events, he will be at a higher risk of developing the disorder. It is this complex interplay between inborn tendencies, family dynamics, culture, and environment that determines how a child will develop. Disregarding this interplay and focusing only on a child's behavior—biting or tantrums, for example—can lead to narrow conclusions, such as "He's just a bad kid" or "He's just looking for attention" or "She can't do anything for herself because her mom is always babying her."

The provider for five-year-old Daniel reported to a counselor that Daniel was a thief. "He steals snacks out of other children's lunch boxes, and I've caught him a few times going into my desk where I keep extra crackers." She said they had talked to him about his stealing again and again for months, but that he would still try to sneak food practically every day. "He's a naughty child who has no regard for others and their property" was her conclusion.

After looking into the child's history and talking with his mother, the counselor reported back to the provider that Daniel had been adopted from Central America when he was eighteen months old. He had been abandoned as an infant and had spent months in a crowded orphanage after he was finally rescued from the streets. At the time he was adopted, he was suffering from severe malnutrition. Understanding the child in context allowed Daniel's provider to see him through totally different eyes. Working together as a team, Daniel's provider, his family, and the counselor were able to help Daniel learn that hunger was a thing of the past and that there were now many loving adults in his life who would make sure he was safe and secure. By stepping back to look at the bigger picture, the provider gained a more accurate and useful understanding of Daniel's behavior. After a few weeks of intense work, Daniel no longer "stole" food.

The causes of challenging behavior in children are usually more complex than what appears on the surface. To better understand this, we will now examine in detail how a child's behavior results from a combination of four basic factors:

- inborn characteristics, such as temperament and genetics
- relationships with family and other caregivers
- culture
- environment

To decide how best to support a child and to gain a deeper understanding of what makes a child tick, all four factors must be taken into account. When you put all this information together, you come to a better understanding of why the child is behaving the way she is and how best to help her.

Inborn Characteristics

While family, culture, and environment play a large part in the emotional development of children, the child also brings something to the mix. Each child is born and grows with a unique set of physical, emotional, and developmental qualities. Children have different temperaments and develop at different paces. Individual differences between children can make it difficult to determine whether a behavior is part of normal development or a symptom of something more concerning. Does the child have a shy temperament or is she depressed? Is the child going through the "terrible twos" at age four or is he showing signs of oppositional defiant disorder? Observation, experience, and knowledge of typical child-development timelines are needed to make sense of atypical behaviors.

PHYSICAL FACTORS

The physical factors that can influence and cause psychological disorders fall into three main categories: pregnancy and birth; heredity; and injuries, illnesses, or disabilities.

Pregnancy and birth. For example, babies born prematurely, those born to mothers who use alcohol or drugs, and those who have low birth weight are at higher risk of developing problem behaviors and psychological disorders.

Heredity. A history of mental illness in the family increases a child's chances of developing mental illness. For example, children with depressed parents have a higher chance of developing depression.

Injuries, illnesses, or disabilities. Children with vision or hearing challenges, speech and language delays, sensory problems, or learning disabilities are at higher risk of developing social or emotional challenges. A child's early experience with an injury or illness—and its lasting effects—can also play a part in behavior. Though these experiences and their effects are not "inborn" qualities, we have included them here because they may affect a child's behavior in much the same way an inborn quality would.

EMOTIONAL QUALITIES

Babies are born with unique temperaments that color how they interact with the world. In any group of children, many behavioral differences based on each child's inborn temperament are readily apparent. A child with a quiet, observant temperament might take a lot of time to observe a playgroup before trying to enter it. A toddler with a more adventurous, outgoing temperament might move right in before figuring out what the other children are playing. A baby who startles easily might cry when the doorbell rings, whereas an easygoing baby might look around with curiosity. Temperament includes some of the qualities and behaviors listed below.

Sensitivity. Does he get upset easily? Does every little sound wake him?

Attention span. Does she gaze into your eyes for a minute or two, or does she immediately turn away? Does her attention flit quickly from one thing to another?

Activity level. Is he always awake and aware and ready to go? Or does he enjoy sitting quietly, watching the world go by?

Distractibility. Does she focus on the task at hand, even when other things are going on around her? Or does she easily get sidetracked by little things that happen nearby?

Intensity of reactions. Does he jump in response to a sudden noise but then easily return to whatever he was doing? Or does he startle easily and begin to cry?

Daily rhythm development. Is she developing a pattern of sleeping, eating, and playing on her own? Or do her hunger and sleepiness appear to be random?

DEVELOPMENTAL QUALITIES

Although there are predictable behaviors that develop concurrently with cognitive, physical, and emotional development, each child develops at his own pace, constantly changing, sometimes moving forward and sometimes moving backward. This week the baby might give up her bottle, but next week she might ask for it again as she begins cutting a new tooth. A child who's been crying when his grandmother drops him off in the morning may soon become attached to his new provider and no longer be distressed when his grandmother departs.

Some developmental discrepancies can be signs of a more serious problem. A typical behavior for a two-year-old, such as biting, might cause concern when the child is four. While tantrums at four might be typical, at thirteen they are not.

Children have unique personal strengths and challenges. A four-year-old child with a knack for language may develop friendships quickly and might evolve into a leader, but a four-year-old child with speech challenges who finds himself left out of dramatic play might decide to quit trying to play with others.

The Social/Emotional Developmental Continuum in Appendix A shows developmental expectations for infants, young toddlers, older toddlers, preschoolers, and prekindergarteners. This continuum provides a guide to the skills children typically develop at certain ages, although each child will move through the stages of skill development at her own pace. Overall, some children will develop slowly, others more quickly. Some will develop rapidly in one area and slowly in another. It is less important that a child reaches a particular milestone at a particular age than that she exhibits a pattern of growth over time. The child should be moving from stage to stage, developing new skills. If a child stagnates at one level for a long period of time or moves further and further backward over the months, it may be time to talk to her parents about getting a professional assessment.

What the Family Brings

Relationships are the building blocks of healthy development. Infants, toddlers, and preschoolers do all their social and emotional learning in relationship with others. The quality of the caregiver-child relationship is one of the biggest factors that influences the overall development and mental health of a child. The child's relationship with his primary caregivers—his parent(s) or guardian(s)—has the greatest influence. If he is in child care or preschool all day (or even half a day) three to five days a week, then his providers or teachers, as secondary caregivers, also have a tremendous influence on him.

The primary caregiving relationship is a two-way street. The match between a caregiver's temperament and a baby's temperament is sometimes called "goodness of fit." A quiet, observant baby may be relaxed with a low-key caregiver but may exhibit a lot of stress with a louder, more exuberant caregiver. An active, alert, and curious baby might enjoy time with a very interactive caregiver but might not do as well with a caregiver who is more passive and quiet.

The nature of the primary and secondary caregiving relationships and the goodness of fit between child and caregiver are particularly important because these repeated interactions can assume patterns and become internalized as "models" or expectations about self, the world, and others. These expectations play a major role in guiding the way the child interacts with the larger world as she develops. Research has shown that early caregiving experiences affect the physical development of the brain, molding neural pathways in the brain that become harder to change over time. A child's relationship with his primary and secondary caregivers has a significant effect on how she thinks about herself, her relationships, and her world.

SELF

Self-esteem and self-efficacy. If a child's caregivers are consistently responsive and nurturing, the child learns that he has value and that others can be depended on for support and comfort. He learns that he can communicate his needs to others and that those needs will usually be met. When children grow up in an environment where their cries for help, food, or comfort receive erratic responses, they likely will come to believe that they are powerless to get their needs met and that they have no value as individuals.

Children may also feel unworthy if caregivers have unrealistic expectations of them. When a caregiver demands, for example, that a two-year-old share her special toy or that a four-year-old learn to "write neatly between the lines," the child is likely to feel confused and discouraged. Or if screaming and threatening are the caregiver's principal means of communicating with a child, the child may, over time, show signs of distress.

Self-regulation. Self-regulation is the basis of early childhood development. At birth, it is up to the child's caregiver to "co-regulate" for the infant, who enters the world with little ability to do this for herself. For example, when a baby is distressed, a caregiver does what she can to figure out what the infant needs, and she tries to soothe the baby. When the baby grabs on too hard to the caregiver's glasses, the caregiver gently moves the child's hand away. She may take the baby outside or find something interesting to catch the baby's attention. Over time, babies and toddlers begin to learn how to soothe themselves, how to control their behavior, and how to focus and pay attention. These three kinds of regulation—emotional, behavioral, and attentional—are required for all other learning and development in the early years.

When a caregiver provides routines, consistent expectations, appropriate soothing experiences, and support to help a baby manage distress, that baby gets the training he needs to begin developing his own regulation skills. If a caregiver's responses are confusing or uncertain, or if the caregiver doesn't help a child manage his natural frustration and distress, the child may have difficulty learning to regulate his emotions. Caregivers who inconsistently set expectations and limits or who fail to consistently enforce limits make it hard for a child to learn the rules and to develop the ability to regulate his behavior.

RELATIONSHIPS

Building supportive and stimulating social relationships is another core necessity for mental health. If a caregiver is emotionally absent or harsh and hurtful, a baby learns that others are not reliable or are to be feared and avoided. Babies reared in such environments may stop looking to communicate with others, and it may be hard to engage them in social activities. On the other hand, babies reared in warm, loving, and supportive environments learn the power and pleasure of communicating with and relating to others and can quickly acquire the communication and social skills specific to their culture. These skills are vital to the development of mental health.

THE WORLD

A child raised by a loving, attentive caregiver is likely to develop different ideas about the nature of the world than a child who is raised by an inconsistent, harsh, or neglectful caregiver. For young children, the home is their world. If the home environment is a kind and gentle place, the child tends to view the world as an inviting place. If the home environment is negative and inconsistent, the child learns to expect inconsistency and harshness from the world at large.

The Role of Culture

We can understand a child's behaviors more completely by looking at those behaviors in the context of the family's cultural traditions. Culture includes all the values, rules, and guidelines that shape how we conduct our lives, our relationships with others, and our interactions with our environment and the world. Cultural traditions influence virtually everything we do, from how we eat to the way we raise our children, from what defines a family or household to our spiritual beliefs, from the rules of etiquette to the expectations and roles for males and females.

Since traditions and norms vary from culture to culture, each of us develops, based on our cultural background, a unique set of expectations about the self, relationships, and the world. Understanding a child's "psychological self" requires understanding a child's "cultural self."

Different cultures vary greatly in how they raise babies. And each family, influenced by the culture in which it lives, has its own beliefs about childrearing practices, what normal development is, what role each person in the family holds in relation to the child, and even what specific behaviors mean. Some cultures promote infants and toddlers sleeping in the same bed with their caregivers, while other cultures encourage separate beds for children at a very early age. Some cultures promote toilet learning at a young age, while others take a more laissez-faire approach. Children in some cultures are expected to learn to feed themselves as early as possible, and in other cultures, mothers spoon-feed their children well beyond the toddler years.

In addition to differing expectations of how quickly children should take on responsibility for personal skills, the meaning associated with different behaviors varies from culture to culture. For example, a young child who asks for a turn on the swing might be applauded by one family for using words to communicate, while another family might reprimand such behavior as too assertive. A boy who hits back when hit by another child may be regarded as strong and manly in one household, while in another household such behavior is seen as violent and inappropriate. A young girl who appears to be overly passive with low self-esteem might in fact be acting in a way that is expected for female children in her home. Without an understanding of the variety in cultural norms, it can be easy to misjudge the meaning of a child's behavior.

> Let's say you ask four-year-old Rosa what is special about her. She answers, "My brothers and sisters." "But," you persist, intending to help Rosa develop a better sense of self-worth, "what's special about you?" Rosa looks at you blankly and answers again, "My brothers and sisters." You are concerned that Rosa is not developing a sense of self. It appears that she doesn't even know she has special or unique qualities.

> But when you look at Rosa in the context of her home and culture, you realize that she is one of seven children in a Latino household, and in her family, children are expected to value kinship over all else. When one child gets a toy or treat, she is expected to share it with her siblings. Putting family first is a cultural norm and expectation for Rosa, and when she is asked about her "specialness," it is healthy and consistent for her to identify her siblings as what makes her special. Rather than low self-esteem, she has a good understanding of who she is in relation to her family and her culture.

Many different childrearing beliefs and traditions promote healthy mental and emotional development. Research informs us, however, that regardless of cultural varieties in childrearing practices, attachment to a significant caregiver is key to a child's healthy development.

What the Environment Brings

A child's environment is the fourth major factor in the development of mental health. Children who attend story time at the library, the local puppet theater, or a bookstore will probably come into a preschool setting with a foundation for and an interest in learning to read. Children who have many opportunities to play outdoors, to run in fields, to climb trees, and to go swimming are more likely to come to school eager to engage in active outside play. On the other hand, children from a home where there are few creative toys and experiences or where TV and electronic games are the main activities will be more challenged in a creative learning environment.

The quality of the child care setting can be a significant environmental factor as well. A preschool or child care center with rich, stimulating learning areas and activities staffed by consistent, responsive providers supports all aspects of a child's development, including emotional development. Frequent provider turnover, inconsistent rules and interventions, and lack of stimulation can all have negative effects on the emotional growth and development of children.

A child's experiences also include nonphysical features, such as the kind of human interactions they have at home, in their neighborhood, and in their community at large. Children whose lives are filled with domestic violence or who regularly witness gang violence, for example, are more likely to be anxious, untrusting, and fearful of interactions with others, or they may be filled with aggression. Witnessing violence can be as traumatic as experiencing violence firsthand. One study shows that a toddler who sees aggression toward his mother is more likely to develop posttraumatic stress disorder (PTSD) than a child who is himself assaulted (Scheeringa and Zeanah 1995).

Other studies show that behavior is different for children who grow up under constant stress, and that stress influences brain development. Chemicals released when the body is under stress bathe the brain, stimulating a child's inborn survival mode. When the brain is continually exposed to these chemicals, its sensitivity to the chemicals changes. Children who experience continuous stress may startle more easily and may react to a harmless accidental bumping as if it were a form of aggression. They may seem never to relax into play, always ready to fight or to flee. Children who witness violence as a regular part of their lives may become desensitized and unconcerned about violence and aggression in general. It follows that the incidence of mental health complications among children who regularly witness violence is extremely high.

You Can Make a Big Difference

As a provider, you fill a powerful role in a child's mental health development. You are in a position to provide both a safe and predictable classroom or child care setting and nurturing relationships. You can increase a child's protective factors by supporting her social relationships, sense of self, self-regulation, communication skills, and social skills. You can help reduce risk factors by working with a child's family and any involved agencies to meet a child's basic physical and emotional needs and to reduce stress. With your knowledge of child development, you may be the first to notice something that's not quite right and to open a dialogue with the child's primary caregivers. Within the healthy emotional environment you have established, you will be able to implement additional strategies to support children with troubling behaviors or with mental health diagnoses.

See Appendix A for a table summarizing the developmental continuum for children from infancy through prekindergarten. The table includes examples of benchmark behaviors for each developmental milestone.

I have yet to see any problem, however complicated, which, when you looked at it in the right way, did not become still more complicated.
—POUL ANDERSON

As long as one keeps searching, the answers come.
—JOAN BAEZ

CHAPTER 2: Observing Children's Behavior for Signs and Symptoms of Mental Illness

Determining a young child's mental health status can sometimes seem like trying to catch a slippery eel in the dark with rubber gloves on. As you've learned, a child's behaviors and mental health are influenced by many things—inborn traits, family, culture, and environment. Behavior that might not seem severe enough to be labeled a "problem" still might seem out of the ordinary. This chapter will help you understand both the process and challenges involved in diagnosing a young child and your role in this process.

What Is a Diagnosis?

Over many years, mental health professionals and scientists have studied the behavior of people considered "mentally ill." They have found that certain symptoms will consistently occur together, thus making up an identifiable disorder. A "diagnosis" is a label describing a group of symptoms that together define a particular disorder. With new research and experience, criteria for a diagnosis change and are refined over time.

For many years, clinicians felt that very young children could not have diagnosable psychological disorders. They thought that young children didn't have the cognitive ability or emotional maturity to experience those kinds of persistent problems. Now we know better—and since early childhood psychology and mental health is a growing and changing field, we still have much to learn.

Mental health clinicians[1] use a resource called the *Diagnostic and Statistical Manual of Mental Disorders*, Fourth Edition, Text Revision (commonly referred to as the DSM-IV-TR), a standard tool compiled by the American Psychiatric Association to help clinicians diagnose mental illness in adults and children. A nonprofit organization, Zero to Three, recently developed a tool to aid in the diagnosis of infants and toddlers, the *Diagnostic Classification of Mental Health and Developmental Disorders of Infancy and Early Childhood*, Revised Edition (commonly referred to as the DC:0–3R); it is meant to supplement the DSM-IV-TR and is considered a work in progress.

A diagnosis helps clinicians understand what a child is experiencing and aids them in developing a treatment plan. In recent years, a diagnosis has become necessary for insurance purposes. Diagnoses also help determine the focus of ongoing research in the field, and they can be helpful to you as a provider. When a child is diagnosed with a specific mental disorder, you can learn what behaviors to expect and how you might best modify your practices to respond to those behaviors.

Mental health personnel, pediatricians, and various support agencies might use one or more standardized screening tools in order to understand a child's needs and behaviors as fully as possible. Some tools require a clinician to seek information about the child from providers and the child's family. Other tools are used exclusively by mental health specialists and require no input from family or secondary caregivers. A family may notify you that their child has been or will be screened with one of these tools, and they may have a copy of screening results sent to you. Screening results may or may not include recommended interventions. Appendix B outlines the most common screening tools.

As noted in the introduction, mental illness in children consists of "serious deviations from expected cognitive, social, and emotional development" (U.S. Department of Health and Human Services 1999). We also mentioned that the phrase "serious deviations" contains several assumptions that are important to consider when thinking about mental illness. For example, an unusual

---

[1] Child psychiatrists (medical doctors), psychologists (PhDs in psychology), social workers and other master's level counselors, and psychiatric nurses and other nurse practitioners.

behavior isn't necessarily a serious deviation if it has happened only once or only at home. Remember, in order to be considered a disorder, the following must also be true:

- The symptoms occur often and last a long time.

- The symptoms are present in more than one setting.

- The symptoms cause significant distress or impairment in functioning or both.

Many factors must be considered before a diagnosis is made. A child in your classroom or child care setting may meet some criteria but not others. Perhaps he has all the symptoms but only for a short period of time or only at school. Maybe she is able to participate and develop appropriately despite struggling with some symptoms. Children who meet some but not all criteria still may need additional support and understanding in the classroom or child care setting, even though they haven't been labeled with a "disorder." A conservative approach to diagnosis is in fact often recommended in order to avoid labeling children or making assumptions about them that may be inaccurate. And a diagnosis can only be made by a qualified mental health professional. Your role as a provider includes communicating concerns about a child's behavior to primary caregivers and encouraging them to seek professional evaluation, if merited.

You may not always be able to convince a primary caregiver to seek evaluation, or the diagnostic process may take a long time. The primary caregiver may withhold information from you or may exclude you from the treatment planning process. Whether the primary caregiver is willing to work closely with you or not, you'll need tools to help children in your care with social/emotional difficulties. Chapters 5 through 12 provide classroom and child care setting strategy suggestions for working with children with specific diagnoses. If you have access to a mental health professional, we recommend that you work together with him or her as a team as you devise and implement any of these strategies.

Although a lot of work goes into making a diagnosis, the diagnosis itself is not the solution to the problem. Rather, it is a starting point for understanding a child's behaviors. Each child is unique and, for best results, interventions should be tailored to the specific child.

CHALLENGES AND STRATEGIES RELATED TO DIAGNOSIS

Prompt and accurate diagnosis of a psychological disorder in a young child is complicated and filled with challenges, as is addressing the behavior typically associated with a disorder. The following text describes some of the biggest challenges you might face and suggests strategies for dealing with them.

Challenge: OUTDATED BELIEFS ABOUT MENTAL ILLNESS AND CHILDREN'S MENTAL HEALTH

In the introduction, we touched on some once-common beliefs or myths about mental illness. Stereotypes and prejudices based on these myths may still persist, making it difficult for young children to get the mental health support they need. Primary caregivers may believe that children cannot have mental health problems or that others will blame *them* for their child's difficulties. They might avoid seeking help because they worry that others will label them or shun them and their child. Perhaps they worry about giving medications to their child or about having to reveal personal and family information they'd prefer to keep private.

Program directors and providers also may have misconceptions about children with mental illness. One provider may demand that an unruly child be medicated in order to remain in the program, while another may be reluctant or feels unqualified to manage a child on medications. Some providers may feel that children with mental health diagnoses should never be mainstreamed and should instead be placed in special programs. Other providers may have personal or cultural prejudices that color their recognition of a disorder and hence influence decisions about whether or not to have a child evaluated.

Strategy

It is important to continue to educate yourself and others about early childhood mental health. Examine some of your own prejudices and misconceptions about mental illness, and be sure you are up-to-date in understanding the causes and appropriate treatments for specific psychological disorders. Appendix D lists resources for educators and families seeking additional information.

Challenge: LIMITATIONS OF CURRENT DIAGNOSTIC CRITERIA

Young children with mental illness often experience the illness differently from older children or from adults with the same disorder. For example, in adults with bipolar disorder, the cycles of elation and depression can take weeks or months, but young children can cycle many times in one day. Because research on young children is rather new, clinicians are more likely to fail to diagnose or to incorrectly diagnose an infant, toddler, or preschooler than an adult. Misdiagnosis can result in incorrect medication or in strategies that may worsen behaviors or further delay getting needed help to the child. As with adults, children may have notable behaviors that do not fit cleanly into a specific diagnostic category. Children may be too young or may not have enough symptoms to be diagnosed. To make matters more difficult, the process of getting a child evaluated and diagnosed often takes months or longer.

Strategy

Even though a child may be too young to get a formal diagnosis or may not yet have a full-blown disorder, you need to commit yourself to understanding and documenting troubling behaviors. Behavior tendencies in early childhood that aren't yet diagnosable as a full-blown psychological disorder can be early signs of serious problems ahead. In fact, half the children who have problem behaviors in preschool continue to have problems in elementary school (Campbell 1995). And, for most children who are diagnosed with problems in elementary and high school, signs of trouble began appearing in early childhood. Older children with conduct disorders, substance abuse problems, depression, violence, and failure in school showed signs of aggression, oppositional defiant disorder (ODD), and noncompliance when they were in preschool. Although some children outgrow troublesome behaviors without any help, others do not.

There is evidence that early support and guidance may help prevent worsening of symptoms and the development of mental health problems. It's important that you pay attention to signs and symptoms, such as aggression, lack of social skills, or poor attachment, when you first see them—whether or not the child receives a formal diagnosis. Keep an eye on signs of distress that don't go away and monitor any regularly occurring behaviors that don't seem quite right (atypical behaviors). Babies and preschoolers sometimes exhibit behaviors that may not be diagnosable mental health problems but are still out of the ordinary. Examples would include a four-month-old who rarely giggles or smiles or a five-year-old who ignores invitations to play. Although such isolated behaviors do not necessarily indicate diagnosable disorders, they are behaviors that should be noted and watched over time. If the child's mental health status is revisited later on, documentation of these behaviors may provide a clinician with the evidence needed to make a diagnosis.

Challenge: ADDRESSING A DIAGNOSIS INSTEAD OF A UNIQUE CHILD

Making assumptions about a child based on a diagnostic label is all too easy. A provider may modify the way she interacts with the child or she may change her expectations for him in ways that lead to self-fulfilling prophecies. For example, if a child has been diagnosed with attention-deficit/hyperactivity disorder (ADHD), adults may not expect him to attend story time. They may allow the child to wander off while the rest of the four-year-olds are expected and encouraged to stay and listen to the story. Such lowered expectation for the child with ADHD may cheat him out of the encouragement he needs to develop a longer attention span. A formal diagnostic label might also narrow the implemented strategies to those traditionally used for a specific disorder.

Strategy

The best strategy for helping a child with a mental illness diagnosis is tailored specifically to that child and takes into account the child's individual strengths and challenges, along with her familial and cultural background. It is a mistake to believe that all children with a given diagnosis will have exactly the same behavior or will need exactly the same intervention. Although, as you will read in Part 2 of this book, children with the same diagnosis share similar traits, individualized intervention is always the best practice in the classroom or child care setting. Try to shift your focus from the diagnostic label (for example, "depression") to the child's behavior (for example, "avoids play with others"). Chapter 3 provides guidelines and suggestions on how to respond to specific behaviors regardless of a formal diagnosis.

Challenge: THE LIMITED ABILITIES OF YOUNG CHILDREN TO USE LANGUAGE TO COMMUNICATE WHAT'S GOING ON WITH THEM

When a clinician uses the DSM-IV-TR to diagnose a client, she relies heavily on what the patient reports about his feelings and experiences. But very young children lack the advanced language skills, abstract-reasoning abilities, and introspective qualities that would allow them to talk about their feelings the way adults can. Children express their feelings more through actions than through words. And, since young children may use one behavior to express many different feelings—for example, aggressive behavior could indicate the child is feeling angry, sad, or frustrated—figuring out exactly what a young child is feeling can be difficult.

Strategy

The more accurate and complete the information a clinician has about a child, the better the chance that the diagnosis will be accurate. Young children rarely have the words to report their own symptoms. Instead, they rely on their caregivers to gather information through observing their behavior, mood, and other traits. For example, two-year-old Elizabeth can't tell you she has lost interest in activities she used to enjoy. But you may observe that her attention span is shorter than usual or that she doesn't respond to your invitations to play in the manner she used to.

As a provider, you're in a wonderful position to observe children and to gather information about their social and emotional development. You are also in a unique position to talk to primary caregivers and mental health professionals about your experiences with, and observations of, a child. Your observations can help families and professionals put together a complete picture of the child. At the end of this chapter, we'll provide specific recommendations for observing and recognizing symptoms.

Challenge: DEVELOPMENTAL FACTORS

The line between typical challenging behavior and behavior that is cause for concern is blurry where infants, toddlers, and preschoolers are concerned. Although there is usually a range or continuum of behavior and accomplishment that is considered typical for a particular age (as discussed in chapter 1), young children are growing, changing, and leaping forward at different rates. Sometimes a child who has shown steady progress across the developmental continuum will regress briefly before moving to the next stage. There is cause for concern only when a child's behavior or development is significantly different from what is expected at that age or when growth is not continuing over time.

Strategy

Concentrate on combining your growing knowledge of the developmental continuum for young children with good observation and documentation skills. Expand your focus from the immediate behavior emergency to take in a broader picture of the child's overall development. For example, instead of focusing exclusively on the fact that Bennie just bit Emily—again—consider the big picture: At age four, Bennie should be able to regulate his emotions and behavior enough not to bite. Bennie has trouble playing with other children. Although he seems to understand what is said to him, he doesn't use much expressive language in communicating with others. He has trouble with transitions and doesn't listen to anyone other than his regular provider.

Challenge: FAMILY AND CULTURAL CONSIDERATIONS

Family expectations and values influence children's behavior. Sasha's family places a high value on dependence, closeness, and obedience. In school, providers describe her as agreeable and very well behaved. She's always asking the teachers if they need help or making special pictures for them. But they worry that she'd rather be with them than run around playing with the other children.

Quang's family values assertiveness, independence, and personal accomplishment. His provider describes him as an active and curious child who is always first to dive into new activities. He's a good kid but often debates with adults when redirected or asked to do something. He's been known to say "You're not the boss of me" when he gets frustrated.

Sasha's focus on the adults in her life is a behavior valued at her home. Quang's assertion and independence are valued in his home.

Strategy

Be aware of your own cultural values and biases when determining if a behavior is a cause for concern or is simply typical for a child from a particular culture. Make an effort to learn something about the child's home life and cultural background, and then take these factors into account as you assess the child's behavior and compare it with the typical emotional and social milestones used to evaluate a child's developmental progress. Understanding how behaviors vary with particular family and cultural practices contributes to a more balanced evaluation of the child's behavior.

Challenge: DIFFERENCES BETWEEN HOME AND CHILD CARE SETTING

A child may act differently at home than at child care or preschool, making it difficult to separate the child's behavior from her relationships in these two environments. Both primary and secondary caregivers may change their own behaviors to adapt to a child's behavior, thereby masking the child's symptoms. For example, three-year-old Courtney was very afraid of strangers. She trembled, wet her pants, and vomited when her parents left her with a babysitter or took her to Sunday school. Her parents decided it was easier not to leave her with strangers, and she stopped showing anxiety around unfamiliar people when she was with her family. When, at age four, she began going to a prekindergarten program, her transition to school in the morning was extremely difficult for her. She wept, she wet, she vomited. Because her family had adapted to her stranger anxiety at home, she no longer behaved like that at home. But school is a different setting, so the behavior came out at school. This diagnosis would be complicated, because one of the requirements for diagnosis of a psychological disorder is that it happens regardless of setting—whether the child is at home or at child care. In this case, family intervention masked the anxiety at home.

Children adapt their behavior to both healthy and unhealthy aspects of their environment and relationships. The same behavior that appears to be a sign of a disorder in the classroom or child care setting might actually serve the child well in a dysfunctional home environment. Behaviors such as tantrums or use of profanity may be learned behaviors, based on a child's environment or on his relationship with primary caregivers. For example, Jorge's mother was disconnected and unresponsive to him as a newborn. During his first year, he learned not to count on adults. At two years old, he discovered he could get his mother's attention by throwing a tantrum. Now, when Jorge needs help or support from any adult, at home or at school, he throws himself on the floor screaming and kicking. This is the only way he knows how to get his basic needs met.

Strategy

To fully understand a young child's behavior, it's important to look at her relationship with her primary caregiver and other family members. This is important not only for diagnosis but also for effective intervention planning. It's easy to lose sight of the importance of the role of the primary caregiver relationship and the need for caregiver involvement in treatment when it's the child who carries a label. As we learned in chapter 1, most disorders are the result of a complex combination of factors, and no factor is more significant than a child's relationship with her primary caregiver. Chapter 4 discusses the nature of the partnership between the primary caregiver and the provider and outlines communication strategies for strengthening the partnership so providers can work together with families for the welfare of the child.

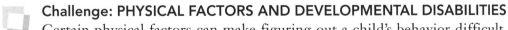

Challenge: PHYSICAL FACTORS AND DEVELOPMENTAL DISABILITIES

Certain physical factors can make figuring out a child's behavior difficult. Children with speech delays, hearing challenges, or issues with motor development might behave in ways that appear to indicate a mental health problem, when actually the behavior has physical causes. If a child who is developmentally ready to make friends and get involved in pretend play has a language delay that makes it hard for him to express his thoughts, his social skills will suffer. While others are using words to set limits, ask for turns, or take roles in pretend play, that child will have trouble keeping up and may resort to physical actions to hitting, pushing, and grabbing in order to communicate. The child may then be misdiagnosed with an emotional disorder even though the root of his undesirable behavior lies with his language limitations. Research has shown that at least 50 percent of children with behavior disorders also have some kind of language disorder.

Strategy

With the right support, most children with physical challenges, developmental delays, or disabilities will develop appropriate social and emotional skills over time. When you observe a problem behavior in a child, first rule out possible physical or developmental reasons for her behavior. For example, observe and listen to the child to discover how well she can communicate what she needs to say (expressive language) and how well she understands what is being said to her (receptive language). Share with primary caregivers any concerns you have regarding a particular child's overall development. Refer families to organizations that provide early screening and identification of such problems. Delays in identification and treatment can result in the development of new behavior challenges or in the worsening of existing ones.

OBSERVATION AND RECOGNITION OF SYMPTOMS

Observing and recognizing symptoms in young children is a difficult task. There are many factors, covered earlier in this book, to keep in mind: a young child's limited language ability, developmental changes, the role of physical and developmental disabilities, family and cultural considerations, and the possibility that dramatic differences may exist between home and child care settings. In addition, each child is unique and complex and needs to be seen and appreciated for all his strengths and challenges without the pigeonholing that can happen with generalization, assumptions, or labeling. The following skill list, along with the social/emotional continuum chart in Appendix A, can help guide your observations.

What to look for: Is the child developing the six basic skills needed for mental health?

1. The child seeks out primary caregivers for companionship, affection, comfort, and support. Is the child attached to a primary caregiver in the home? Has the child been able to identify an adult in the program as a significant

adult to rely on in the absence of the primary caregiver? Does the child initiate and respond to interactions with significant adults?

2. The child looks for companionship, connection, and community from peers and others outside the household. Does the child show interest in and seek to be near other children? Does the child initiate and respond to invitations to interact with other children?

3. The child is learning to regulate emotions, behavior, and attention. Can the child comfort herself? Does she accept assistance and redirection from significant adults to help her regulate behaviors? Can she focus on an activity?

4. The child is developing the communication and social skills needed to interact with others. Can the child make her presence known? Can she communicate her feelings to others? Is she learning the cultural expectations of social interactions?

5. The child recognizes that he can do things, make things happen, and solve problems (self-efficacy). Does the child recognize his own abilities? Is he persistent? Does he get pleasure from exploration and achievement?

6. The child is developing an understanding of self and relationship to others. Is the child recognizing herself as an individual and recognizing others as individuals as well? Is the child learning to respond to the feelings and needs of others?

When to observe: The regular daily schedule and activities of a program provide many opportunities to observe how well a child relates to significant adults and peers, her abilities to self-regulate, her communication and social skills, her self-efficacy, and her growing awareness of self and others. Some examples of good times to observe follow.

1. Separation and reunion times with family members provide information on adult-child bonding and self-regulation.

2. Toileting, eating, and sleeping times let you observe the development of behavior regulation and self-efficacy.

3. Setting-based free-play times provide good opportunities to observe a child's desire to play with others, as well as his self-regulation, self-efficacy, communication and social skills, and self-awareness.

4. Transition times are when you're most likely to notice children who are struggling with self-regulation.

5. During teacher-led small and large group activities you can note a child's response to adults, behavior and attention regulation, communication and social skills, and understanding of self and others.

6. To gather valuable information about a child's development of behavior regulation skills, compare how well a child functions in structured, routine times of the day compared with more-unstructured times.

Reflect on your observations. As you reflect on your observation notes, be alert for the following:

1. Behaviors that are atypical or unexpected based on age and developmental phase. Use Appendix A as a quick reference. Also take into account the impact of family dynamics, norms and expectations, culture, and the broader environmental context.

2. Behaviors that happen frequently and over a long period of time. Every child has a bad day or even a bad week or two. And a child sometimes goes through a short regressive phase. Pay special attention to behaviors that persist beyond natural ups and downs.

3. Behaviors that create difficulties in several areas of the child's life. Does the child have the same difficulties with different caregivers or in different settings, such as at home and at school? Does the problem touch many areas of the child's life, or are the problems linked with a certain caregiver or setting?

4. Behaviors that get in the way of the child being successful in school and life. For example, is she failing to learn or to develop age-appropriate social skills? Is he unable to follow basic limits and expectations of the classroom or to participate in regular daily activities?

Document your findings. As you summarize and document your findings, you may find that you need to go back and observe certain behaviors more closely to fill in all the details, including:

1. When does it happen? In the morning? At the end of the day? During circle time? When someone leaves the classroom? During certain types of activities? With certain peers? During naptime? Transition time? Meals? Unstructured time?

2. How often does it happen? Record how many times the behavior occurs over the course of the day/week.

3. How long does it last? Make a note of the length of time the behavior lasts. Is it a two-minute tantrum or an hour of out-of-control screaming?

4. What seems to trigger the behavior? What is happening right before the behavior starts? What is the child doing? With whom is the child interacting and what is the nature of that interaction?

5. What happens in response to the behavior? How do the other children react? How does the provider react? What is the effect of these reactions on the child?

6. When does the child not exhibit this behavior? What are the circumstances that allow the child to be successful? More structure? More feedback? Different types of activities? Distance from certain peers? Closeness to a provider? Different outcomes or consequences?

This process of observation and documentation will help you better understand the child, better determine the child's needs, confidently discuss your concerns with caregivers, and provide valuable information to the child's clinician or treatment team.

CHAPTER 3: Classroom and Child Care Setting Strategies

Whether or not a child has a formal diagnosis, your task is to respond to the child's behavior in the most supportive way possible. As quoted in an article on the American Psychiatric Association's HealthyMinds Web site, David Fassler, MD, has noted: "If left untreated, the physical, emotional, social and intellectual development of children with mental disorders will be severely stunted, if not crippled. These children are at a heightened risk for school failure and dropout, drug abuse, and many other difficulties—all of which can be prevented by timely evaluation and appropriate treatment" (American Psychiatric Association 2006).

Working with children who have behavioral or mental health challenges involves a team effort. Research has shown that the best results come from a partnership between the school, the family, and mental health professionals. Primary caregivers, providers, and health professionals each play a vital role in the mental health of a child. Providers and caregivers observe and refer; doctors diagnose and advise caregivers on treatment options; caregivers decide on treatment options; and providers address behaviors in the classroom or child care setting.

What providers do in the classroom or child care setting should not be confused with therapy. The provider's role is to help the child use appropriate behavior while decreasing use of inappropriate behavior and to provide an environment conducive to the improvement of the child's overall mental health. The general strategies listed below can serve as a foundation for the more specific strategies discussed throughout the rest of this chapter and the diagnosis-specific strategies covered in Part 2.

- Modify the physical and emotional environment to provide a healthy backdrop for the child to develop and improve her ability to thrive.

- Examine and modify your own relationship with the child based on observation and assessment of his unique and special needs. Mental health for children is greatly influenced by the quality of the child's relationships with significant adults and with peers. Supporting a child with mental health challenges means making individualized adjustments in the way you interact with that child (Zero to Three 2005).

- Support the child's relationships with peers by fostering the development of social language and social interaction skills and by facilitating the child's interactions with other children.

Guiding Principles for Classroom and Setting Strategies

CREATE INDIVIDUALIZED PLANS

A strategy that views a child as a unique individual and is based on observation can best support a child's growth. Once you gather information about a child through observation, research, and family input, you can design within your setting effective support systems tailored for that specific child.

Identify and build on a child's existing strengths. Avoid focusing too much on the "problems," so that the child doesn't begin seeing himself as a problem. Don't let the behavior challenges define the child. He's not an "autistic child" but a "child with autism"; not a "depressed child" but a "child with depression." Focus attention on developmental and behavior goals instead of being overly concerned about pinning a diagnostic label on the child. Your efforts to help a child move easily through transitions will contribute more to the child's mental health improvement than attempting to label him, for example, as "ADHD."

BE CULTURALLY SENSITIVE

Just as a thorough mental health assessment must take into account a child's culture, an intervention strategy should be culturally responsive to an individual child and her family. As mentioned earlier, what is normal for one family could be seen as dysfunctional by another. In the same sense, an intervention that is appropriate for one family might be uncomfortable for another. For example, in an attempt to help a parent bond with her child, we might suggest getting down on the floor to play with the baby. However, in some cultures, sitting on the floor is inappropriate for an adult. By keeping lines of communication open, alternate paths for reaching the same goals can be explored.

BUILD STRONG BONDS WITH CHILDREN

The first step toward helping a child is to establish a warm and safe relationship with her. Here are some basic strategies that help build such bonds between adults and children.

Show personal interest. Connect with children on a personal level to build relationships and attachment. Showing personal interest can help a child feel recognized and worthy. You don't need to spend much time to make this happen. One or two lines of conversation about a child's interests, strengths, or life outside of the classroom or child care setting can have a big impact. Try asking the child about her new puppy, or comment on her skill at riding a trike. Welcome a child in the morning by saying, "Marta, I'm so happy you came to school with us today." It doesn't take much.

Spend five minutes a day. Set up five uninterrupted minutes a day to personally connect with each child one-on-one. With an infant, you might spend this time simply rocking the child in your arms while singing a lullaby (great singing voice not required!).

With a toddler, you may spend this time sitting on the floor near her, letting her take the lead in play. For example, if she's playing a dump-and-fill game with cars and a bucket, you could pick up your own bucket and cars and begin talking about what you're doing. You might say something like, "I'm putting cars in my bucket just like you. Oops, you dumped yours out. Let me try to do that too." Some toddlers enjoy this mirroring type of play, while others may allow you to join into their own play.

Try inviting an older child to interact with you in an activity you know he enjoys. For example, you might ask if he'd like to look at the new shark book with you, or if he'd like to help you fill the water table, or if he wants to shoot baskets with you during outdoor time. Whatever activity he chooses, make sure you totally focus your attention on the child for at least five uninterrupted minutes.

Use active listening. One of the most effective bonding experiences for a child (and for adults too!) is to feel understood by another person. Active listening is a way to communicate that you are sincerely listening to the other person, not only to her words but also to the important message behind her words. Active listening builds strong bonds between people. A child who feels her words are being heard feels more connected to her provider and is much more responsive to guidance than a child who feels alienated.

> *Mr. Ali had set up Candy Land on a small table as an activity choice during free time. Emil and George rushed over to be the first to play. Mr. Ali spent a few minutes teaching the children how to play the game before moving on to help at the art center. A few minutes later, he heard shouting coming from the game table and came over to investigate. "Emil threw all the Candy Land on the floor. He wrecked it and I was winning and now he messed it up," George complained. "It's a stupid game," Emil said defiantly, folding his arms across his chest. This was far from the first time Emil had exhibited disruptive behavior in the classroom.*

When Emil said it was a stupid game and threw the pieces on the floor, what was he trying to say? Did he really just dislike this game, or was he trying to communicate something bigger? Was he struggling to understand the game? Was he feeling inadequate because he has a need to always win and someone else had caught on faster? Or did he simply not find the game all that interesting?

Consider the difference between these two possible ways of responding to this incident:

> *"Fine, Emil," Mr. Ali said firmly. "It might be a stupid game, but you can't throw toys in this room. You've lost your chance to play here now. Put the game back on the table and find something else to do." Emil kicked at the game, and a few pieces skidded across the floor. "I'm gonna throw this stupid game in the trash." Mr. Ali continued, "I'm not going to put up with your nonsense. You can pick it up now, or you can pick it up while the others are outside. Your choice." Emil kicked at the pieces one more time before storm-*

ing off to the art area, where he purposely bumped against Luis and messed up his painting.

Sending a child away from an activity certainly seems to solve the problem for the moment. But beginning an intervention with active listening accomplishes much more. It helps a child with externalizing behavior regain control, it strengthens adult-child bonds, and it helps develop the building blocks and skills for understanding and managing strong emotions.

With active listening, the scene might instead unfold like this:

Mr. Ali knelt down and gently said, "You weren't having fun playing Candy Land?" Emil answered, "It's stupid." "I see. You don't like this game," Mr. Ali continued. "No," Emil said. "Every time George gets the good cards with the pictures and I just get red ones." Mr. Ali drew Emil in and put his arm around his shoulder. "You wanted to get those special cards," he said. As they talked, Emil's body began to relax and his voice sounded less stressed. "You were excited to play and then it wasn't as fun as you thought," Mr. Ali said, beginning to pick up the pieces. "Let's get these back on the table," he said to Emil, now that the child was calmed down. As they worked together picking up the game, Emil said, "I don't want to play this anymore. I want to go to the art table." "Okay. As soon as we have it picked up, you can move on. Maybe you can try Candy Land another time, and maybe you'll get some of those good cards next time," Mr. Ali said, giving Emil a hug.

At first glance, you might think that Mr. Ali gave Emil appropriate consequences in the first scenario and that Emil "got away" with poor behavior in the second. But notice that at the end of the first scenario, Emil not only hadn't cleaned up the game, he'd destroyed the work of another classmate. This incident might have led to a bad day for Emil, who might have continued taking out his lingering frustration on others over the next few hours. And forcing the issue of picking up might have led to even more violence and destruction.

In the second scenario, Emil picked up the game he threw (behavioral regulation), with Mr. Ali's help, and he gained insight into what triggered his behavior and was able to de-escalate his frustration (emotional regulation). The guidance and feedback from Mr. Ali built relationship bonds and helped increase Emil's skill base he needs to be socially and emotionally successful.

Externalizing and Internalizing Behaviors

When thinking about the best way to respond to children's behaviors in the classroom or child care setting, it can be helpful to identify those behaviors as either externalizing or internalizing. Categorizing behaviors in this way can often be more helpful than simply looking at a child's diagnosis. One child's depression might be expressed with externalizing behaviors such as hitting others, while another child with depression might use internalizing behaviors such as passivity. To be most successful, each child needs a different approach from providers.

EXTERNALIZING BEHAVIORS

Externalizing behaviors are commonly seen in children diagnosed with attention-deficit/hyperactive disorder (ADHD), oppositional defiant disorder (ODD), or bipolar disorder. Some common externalizing behaviors of young children include acting out, being defiant, not complying, and being aggressive. These children may have trouble sharing space and playthings, entering play, moving through transitions, dealing with the unexpected, or solving social conflict. Considered below are some strategies for managing externalizing behaviors most productively.

Help children feel organized, and avoid overstimulation. Many children who are aggressive or who have problems with self-regulation are sensitive to their physical environment. Chaos, noise, or an abundance of visual stimulation can increase undesirable behaviors. Clearly defined interest areas reduce overstimulation and help children with attention and self-regulation. Some steps you can take to create such an environment include:

- Provide personal cubbies to help children feel safe and organized.

- Set up a quiet area where children can retreat to calm themselves or to be alone.

- Minimize strong auditory and visual stimulation in the room, which may be too much for some children to handle.

- Avoid the use of music as background noise.

- Cover storage and provider supply areas.

- Carefully arrange wall displays to be aesthetically pleasing, and leave empty wall space between displays.

Help children succeed. Children with externalizing behaviors often develop a self-image of being a problem child. To turn this self-fulfilling prophecy around, these children need to experience successful interactions with others. One way to foster success is to stop potential problem behaviors before they start. Observe a child to discover what triggers the inappropriate behavior. Is it the anxiety of a transition? Is it the child's inability to successfully enter ongoing play with other children? Once you have identified the trigger events, use them as teachable moments when you can move in to support the child emotionally and redirect her to more successful behavior. For example, if you have a child who regularly hits other children during transitions, you might make her your partner during cleanup so that you can model appropriate behavior and help reduce her level of anxiety from all the activity.

Closely monitor busy social areas. Areas such as blocks or dramatic play can be particularly overstimulating for some children. Children with the lowest levels of self-regulation, the lowest play skill-levels, and the lowest communication skill-levels are most likely to have trouble meeting behavior expectations and social norms in the block and dramatic-play areas. The challenge of negotiating space and playthings in the midst of communication demands create stress for these children and may cause them to become aggressive or to feel so anxious that they leave the area. Rather than chasing such children away from these areas, join into the play so you can coach and model successful interactions. Children who are banned from these areas lose valuable practice opportunities to learn social skills and language. Try shadowing a child during times when you expect problems, such as during a transition. Take the opportunity to be by the child's side to model appropriate behaviors and to redirect inappropriate behaviors before they get out of control.

Help children feel that the world is predictable. A child who exhibits externalizing behaviors often acts out more often when she's experiencing a lot of inconsistency in her life. Her behavior can be a way to try to figure out limits and expectations. Young children are motivated by knowing what is expected of them ahead of time and by being able to predict what will happen next. When you establish predictable routines and sequences throughout the day, children are less anxious and exhibit more self-regulation. Routines are particularly useful for transition times and large group times. Visual reminders, such as photos or drawings on the walls, help children learn routines and sequences. For example, you might take photos of children in the classroom or child care setting doing each of the hand-washing steps and then post the photos near the sink where children can see them. Or, if you have a child who seems to feel lost during transitions and expresses his anxiety with aggressive behavior, you might give him a predictable task or responsibility, such as putting all the chairs back in place after an activity or a meal.

Help children learn what behavior you expect. Avoid the defiance and power plays of children with externalizing behaviors by establishing clearly understood and consistent guidelines for behavior within the program. Trouble often arises with these children when they feel personally attacked, such as when the provider attempts to redirect their behavior. To head off defiant reactions, avoid the word "don't" and state expectations in the positive. Tell children what you want them to do rather than what not to do.

Establishing very few but very clear guidelines can also help minimize the frequency of confrontations. For example, when a child hits someone, instead of saying, "Don't hit" (which can feel like a personal attack) or "I don't want to see you hitting anyone anymore" (which can feel like a "me against you" challenge), say instead, "In this room, we use words to talk to others, not hands." Stating guidelines like this (what we call Rules of the Universe) in the first-person plural avoids setting up a child for defiance.

Use language and strategies that let children know you're working in partnership with them. For example, use the word "come" instead of "go" to communicate this partnership to a toddler. Instead of saying, "Go wash you hands," say, "Come, let's wash hands," and lead the child to the sink. When a child makes a mistake or causes harm, use language to communicate support and mentorship. For example, when a child knocks another child's lunch plate off the table, say something like "Uh-oh. Let's figure out how to fix this."

Make sure that you have a child's attention when you talk with her and that she understands the rules. Rules can be reviewed regularly and practiced during circle time as a way to help children learn and understand them.

Providers complained that out on the playground Rebecca continually dumped sand on other toddlers' heads. When the director came in to observe, she noticed that right after Rebecca threw sand, she would look around. Oftentimes, the providers were busy with other children and didn't notice what had happened. When the providers became aware that they were responding inconsistently to Rebecca, they assigned one provider, Ms. D, to keep her eye on Rebecca for the next week or so. The first day, Ms. D caught Rebecca throwing sand four times. Each time she responded by telling Rebecca "Sand stays on the ground" and then moving her to another area of the yard for a short time. When Ms. D redirected Rebecca, she was careful to tell her

"Sand stays on the ground," rather than "Don't throw sand." She knew that "Don't throw sand" and "Throw sand" get computed in the same way in the brains of toddlers. Also, the provider was calm and neutral in her tone of voice. She did not get irritated or flustered.

The next day, Rebecca threw sand six times, each time looking up to see if a provider was watching. Ms. D responded immediately and consistently. Over the next few days, Rebecca threw sand less and less often. A week later, there was a day with no sand throwing at all.

As Ms. D worked with Rebecca to reduce sand throwing, she consciously gave Rebecca positive feedback when she played appropriately with the sand. She came over from time to time to play a moment with her, and she smiled at her when Rebecca tried to catch her eye.

Help children learn how to have a friend and be a friend. A child with a history of aggressive or impulsive behavior loses opportunities to learn friendship skills from his peers when a provider sends him away from other children because of his aggression or when other children exclude him from play. A lack of opportunity to play peacefully with others serves only to put a child further and further behind during the very important time from three to five years old, when so much social learning happens. All young children need to know how to enter play and how to solve social problems such as sharing materials and space. Support children as they interact with others by giving them the words to enter play, by practicing and role-playing with them, and by coaching them as they try new skills. Help children learn to wait, to take turns, to understand the verbal and physical cues of adults and kids, and to accept the support of others.

In the same way you might teach any other concept, you can teach friendship skills through modeling; by offering opportunities to rehearse, practice, and role-play; and through supportive feedback and coaching. When conflicts inevitably arise, use the conflict resolution procedure on the following page to resolve them. If you use this model on a regular basis, the process will become habit. Guide children to use this model when you yourself are having a conflict with a child, as in the example that follows.

Conflict Resolution Procedure

1. Allow each child to briefly talk and be heard about the issue. Listen, but don't get involved in the back story, and end this piece with, "What is it that you want?"

2. Clarify the problem: "It looks like two kids both want _____" (neutral problem statement).

3. Brainstorm solutions: Have children suggest solutions. Guide them to talk to each other. If they get stuck, say, "I once knew some kids who decided to _____."

4. Select and implement one solution; commit to finding a win-win solution.

5. Congratulate the children for having worked toward finding a solution.

6. Check back to see if the solution worked.

(adapted from "Problem Solving and Conflict Resolution" in *Beyond Behavior Management*, by Jenna Bilmes)

Notice how the teacher in the following incident uses some basic conflict resolution techniques (specified in parentheses) to help Bernie work through what could have been a frustrating experience for everyone.

> *Bernie was playing at the water table when the teacher rang the chime signaling transition to clean-up and outdoor time. Although the other children began to clean up, Bernie continued making tornados. The teacher came over and got down to Bernie's level to give him one-on-one guidance, telling him it was time to put the water tools back into the tub. Bernie angrily picked up a toy in each hand and threw them both on the floor, yelling, "Leave me alone."*
>
> *The teacher touched his arm and gently said, "You're disappointed that water play is over." (Reflect and validate feelings.)*
>
> *Bernie said, "I don't want to clean up. I want to stay here." (Allow the child to express wants/needs.)*
>
> *The teacher said, "You wish you could stay inside, but it's time to go outside. That's a problem." (Clarify the conflict with a neutral problem statement.)*

Bernie complained, "Why do I have to go outside?"

The teacher said, "You want to play with water, and we have to go outside now. I wonder what we can do to solve that problem." (Guide the child to move to problem-solving mode and to brainstorm solutions.)

Bernie said, "Can I take the tornado bottle outside with me?"

"Okay," said the teacher. "Let's get the rest of the water toys picked up and put away, and you can keep the tornado bottle on this table so you can remember to take it out when we go." (Solution is suggested and tried.)

Bernie and the teacher gathered up the rest of the toys, and Bernie took the tornado bottle out with him. (Suggested solution has worked.)

"You figured out a good solution to the problem," said the teacher. (Acknowledge the child for working toward a solution.) Bernie smiled, proud of his accomplishment.

Help children want to behave in appropriate ways. An unfortunate side effect for a child with externalizing behaviors is that her behavior often earns her focused attention from adults and children. Constant negative feedback from others then becomes part of her self-image as the "bad" one. Changing this self-image and helping a child become motivated to use different strategies for attention is a lengthy process. Motivation is a powerful tool for guiding children in developing or changing behaviors. Often we attempt to motivate children with the threat of punishment or by offering rewards for good behavior—this kind of motivation is called extrinsic motivation. Helping children develop intrinsic motivation is a more powerful strategy. *Intrinsic motivation* means helping children develop skills and attitudes to *want* to do what they need to do, without reward or punishment. Although individual children are intrinsically motivated in different ways, the following list provides examples to get you started.

- Build on children's interests. Help children engage in activities they might typically avoid by weaving in themes that interest them. For example, if a child is reluctant to transition from indoors to outdoors, ask him to carry out the spray bottles (which you know he likes to use).

- Give children choices. When children feel they have some control, they're often more willing to comply with expectations. For example, a child who resists lying down to rest might be more motivated if you ask which stuffed animal she'd like to sleep with or which side of the cot she'd like to put her head on.

- Use photos of children to guide behavior. When children see themselves as successful, they tend to act more successful. When a child struggles with a behavior, such as sharing, take a photo of him being successful and post it on the wall. For many children, seeing themselves sharing in a photo increases their motivation to share again.

- Use "strive up" language. Instead of saying, "Stop throwing that water around or you'll have to leave the water table," try "I wonder if you're a kid who can keep the water in the water table." Children with defiant or oppositional behaviors often respond better to a playful challenge than to a direct command.

- Give children positive reflective feedback. Smile at children when they are meeting expectations. Most children strive to behave in ways that get attention and love from significant adults in their lives. Giving attention and reflective feedback when children are *not* exhibiting externalizing behaviors is one of the most effective ways to help them act more appropriately. Most children crave being seen and recognized by adults. Whenever a child gets attention for a behavior, he is more likely to repeat that behavior. Recognizing children when they are complying with expectations motivates them to comply even more. When giving positive feedback, describe to the child exactly what it is about what she's doing that you are noticing. For example, when a baby is eating her food instead of throwing it on the floor, you might smile and say, "Look! I see you are eating all by yourself!"

Sometimes it is effective to ignore inappropriate behaviors. Recognition invites repetition. Anytime we respond to a behavior, it is more likely to be repeated. This is true even when we put a child in time out or scold her. When a behavior isn't dangerous to the child or to other children or property, it is sometimes more effective to ignore the undesirable behavior deliberately. This is especially useful when the child is misbehaving to get attention or to be held. When you first deliberately ignore a child, she may initially increase the inappropriate behavior. It's as if she is thinking, "Hey, didn't you notice me being bad? Let me do it again so you can see me." When deliberately ignoring a child, be very conscious about giving the child an extra dose of attention at other times of the day. Deliberately ignoring without making sure to attend to positive behaviors can leave a child feeling invisible and worthless, making things worse. And while planned ignoring can reduce undesirable behaviors, it's still important to model, teach, coach, practice, and recognize the behaviors you want the child to use instead.

Help children learn to reflect on their behavior. The impulsivity of children with externalizing behavior causes them to act without thinking. Guide these children to reflect on their behavior afterward. Through reflection, they can begin to build the thought processes they need to put a moment of thought between feelings and actions. Use "what" and "how" questions rather than "why" questions. Most young children do not yet have the developmental and cognitive capacity to appropriately answer "why." For example, you might say, "What were you trying to get when you pushed Dasia?" or "How do you think you might get a turn with the red bike?" Helping children learn to reflect provides them with the questions and skills they'll need in order to make conscious decisions about behavior choices.

INTERNALIZING BEHAVIORS

Internalizing behaviors are commonly seen in children diagnosed with anxiety disorders, depression, and bipolar disorder. Some common internalizing behaviors of young children include crying, clinging, fearfulness, withdrawal, stomachaches, avoiding play with others, and an "I can't do it" attitude. These children may have trouble getting involved in activities, coping with change, or showing the typical joyfulness we expect of children. Following are some strategies to manage internalizing behaviors most productively.

Help children manage feelings and communicate their emotions to others. Children who internalize often feel alone. They think they're the only ones who have the feelings they have and that there's something wrong with them. Give children words to describe their feelings—what can be named can be managed. Read to them storybooks with characters that experience fear or anger or sadness, and invite them to talk about similar feelings they may have had. The ability to communicate to others is important for children who internalize, since they often tend to withdraw from relationships.

Help children feel capable. Children with internalizing behaviors often say things like "I can't do it" or "I'm stupid." Work with children to develop "expert charts." In large or small groups, have each child identify an area in which she is an expert. Gather this information on a wall chart or in a class-made book. When possible, include photos of the children demonstrating their expertise. For example, one child may be an expert at bike riding, another at setting the table for snack, and another at hopping on one foot. A child who internalizes, such as a child with depression, may have trouble identifying her expertise. Guide her with statements such as "Yesterday I saw you printing your name on your artwork. I think you might be a printing expert," or "You listen so carefully when we read stories. I think you might be a listening expert."

An older child might benefit from an "I Can" journal. Every few days, take out the journal and guide him in reflecting on his recent achievements and successes. To prompt his memory, you might use photos of him. You're looking for little things here, such as "I built a tall tower with the blocks" or "I petted the hamster" or "I cooked my project at the cooking table." Make sure the child has access to the journal, send it home for him to share with his family, and look through it with him during quiet times when you have a free moment.

Help children feel hopeful. Children with internalizing behaviors often feel that nothing is fun or worth looking forward to. Some activities that can help children feel more hopeful include:

- Getting children involved in planning activities for the future, such as a field trip.

- At the end of the day, reminding children of something fun coming up the next day.

- Keeping photo albums of fun times and special events for children to look at by themselves or with a special grownup.

Help children feel a sense of structure. Depressive behaviors increase when children feel a lack of structure. Regular, predictable routines help children feel more in control of their world. What may feel boring and repetitive to us can help soothe an anxious or depressed child.

Help children feel connected. Children who internalize may avoid social contacts with adults or peers. To help draw them into comfortable interactions with others:

- Encourage socializing through buddy projects and buddy jobs.

- Invite the child to share a two-person riding toy.

- Set up as a center a two-person snack table.

- Ask the child to help you move a table or to help you carry some books.

- Set up a "waiting chair" at the computer, to turn computer time into a two-person activity.

- Develop social rituals. Like routines, social rituals are soothing for children and help reduce anxiety. Rituals provide pleasurable feelings and can motivate young children. For example, if toddlers leaving the playground to go inside all stop to wave and say, "Bye-bye, playground. See you later," it can help them feel more connected and make the transition inside easier. Singing the same greeting song at morning meeting each day is another example of a ritual useful for calming and connecting children.

Help children manage fears. The key to helping children cope with fears is to validate their feelings, play-act, help them make sense of their feelings, and, if possible, avoid reinforcing their fears.

Aayala screamed in panic every time there was a fire drill. Providers dreaded the monthly practice. Aayala's panicky feelings became so intense that she would begin screaming when providers warned her ahead of time that the alarm would go off. The providers consulted their mental health specialist to find out if taking Aayala outside before the alarm sounded might help her. But the specialist thought that avoiding the fire alarm might actually reinforce Aayala's fear. Instead, the specialist suggested that one of the providers tape-record the alarm noise. The provider then sat with Aayala beside the recorder and said, "That alarm sounds very scary, doesn't it?" Then she showed Aayala how to push the play button and the stop button to turn the recorder on and off. She also showed Aayala how to use the volume knob to turn the noise up and down. Aayala was fascinated with the recorder and was able to tolerate the alarm noise. Next time there was a fire drill, the provider took Aayala to the front office where the alarm switch was triggered. Aayala was able to help the director pull the switch. She was still startled by the noise but was able to stay calm in the arms of her provider. Within a few months, although Aayala was still startled when the alarm went off, she didn't panic as long as a provider was nearby.

Medications

Some children in your class may be taking medication for diagnosed mental disorders. Medication is an important part, but only one part, of a comprehensive treatment plan. And even the best medications don't eliminate all symptoms and difficulties. A child also needs your help and support with behavior in the classroom or child care setting. In addition, you'll need to understand a few basics about medication use with children:

- The physician is the expert on medications, and the family is the expert on the child. The decision whether or not to medicate is made by the treating physician and the family. It is inappropriate for care providers to attempt to coerce a family to medicate their child or to stop using medication against their physician's advice.

- Medication must be taken in the correct dosage at the correct time. Many medications must be given on a specific schedule in order to be effective. Failing to receive a dose or getting medication too early or too late can cause medications to be less effective and can produce troubling side effects.

- Observed changes in a child's behaviors should be reported to the family. Providers should be on the lookout for a decrease in symptoms, improvement in the child's functioning, and possible side effects.

Appendix C includes a chart outlining some of the more common psychiatric medications prescribed for children. The most common reasons for using these medications are listed (although doctors will sometimes prescribe these medications for purposes other than those listed), along with some of the most common side effects. If you notice any side effects, be sure to let families know so they can notify their health care provider.

When love and skill work together, expect a masterpiece.
—JOHN RUSKIN

CHAPTER 4: Partnering with Families

Families are essential partners in delivering mental health services for children. Your efforts to develop open, supportive, and mutually respectful relationships with the families of children in your setting or classroom will improve the chances of success for children who need services. Work to establish comfortable and effective communication. Learn about the primary caregivers' hopes and dreams for their child. Ask about their values, beliefs, and expectations. Share your own expectations and child development perspectives with caregivers. Work together as a team to support families' goals for their children. A good adage to remember is "Do unto caregivers as you would have caregivers do unto their children."

Be intentional about the ways you relate to families about their children. The way you interact with caregivers influences the way that caregivers interact with their children. This phenomenon is called *parallel process*. When you use a strength-based, supportive approach, caregivers are more likely to look for the positive in their child and to use supportive rather than punitive strategies. When you approach caregivers with blame, they may in turn approach their child with blame.

Developing Caregiver-Provider Connections

Working together as a therapeutic team with families is one of the key components in working successfully with a child. The child exists as a part of that caregiver-child relationship. Improving the quality of relationships both in school and at home can positively affect a child's behavior in both environments.

BASIC STRATEGIES FOR BUILDING GOOD RELATIONSHIPS WITH CAREGIVERS

Acknowledge and respect diversity, both within cultures and between cultures. Learn to appreciate values, beliefs, and behaviors different from your own.

Approach families with a desire to learn. Attempt to see the child and the world from the family's point of view. Nurturing a child can be different in different cultures. Learn how the family defines and expresses nurturing. Find out who makes childrearing decisions for the family. Is it the mother or the father, or is it one of the elders?

Communicate with the family often. Be available to chat briefly when the caregiver drops off or picks up the child. Share with the family on a regular basis a child's successes and positive experiences. If the primary caregivers have concerns, set up a private time for a focused conversation. Send home "happy notes." Invite the family to help out in the classroom or child care setting or to come along on field trips.

Remember that each family has its own cultural traditions that guide relationships. Increase your effectiveness by learning these traditions. For example, find out the proper way to address adults: Does the family expect the use of a formal system of address in conversations with outside professionals? Does family tradition require sharing hospitality in the form of food, drink, and informal conversation before discussing more serious matters?

Be aware of differences in communication styles. A *low-context* communication style leans toward direct, verbal communication. A *high-context* style, on the other hand, communicates just as much, if not more, through body language, storytelling, and nuance. Ms. Browne, a provider, believed that some of Maria's problems at school would go away if Maria could arrive at school the same time every day, and she shared these concerns with Maria's mother during a home visit. Maria's mother nodded yes when Ms. Browne explained the importance of regular hours. Thinking everything was agreed on, Ms. Browne was annoyed and frustrated that Maria still didn't arrive at school at a regular time. What she wasn't aware of is that in Maria's culture nodding "yes" means "I hear you" and not "I agree with you." If the provider and caregiver use two different styles of communication, it can lead to misunderstandings or hurt feelings.

SHARING CONCERNS WITH FAMILIES

Remember that significant cultural differences exist. How family members talk with nonfamily members about personal problems and how they work with mental health professionals differs from culture to culture. Explore, acknowledge, and validate these attitudes and concerns in order to be as effective as possible when communicating with caregivers. Many providers approach children's challenges with a "fix-it" perspective, but many cultural traditions value a different approach. Instead of looking to current research and new medications to "fix" a child, some traditions are more centered on history and harmony, with an emphasis on accepting and integrating the child into the family as he or she is. People from these cultures may not attach as much importance as you do to new research or techniques. Although this may be difficult for you to understand or accept, it is important to respect a family's way of viewing and nurturing their child. Work together with the family to explore all options, with the best interests of the child and her development in mind.

Use respectful, strength-based language. When talking with primary caregivers about their child, be supportive and warm. You might feel critical and angry with caregivers if you're struggling with their child in the classroom or child care setting, but communicating this frustration will get in the way of establishing a cooperative relationship. Monitor your word choices and tone of voice when conveying concerns. Empathize with caregivers about the challenges of raising children while managing a busy or stressful life. Instead of saying "You're just going to have to get him to bed at a decent hour," try saying "It can be challenging to find the time to do everything that needs to be done in the evening." When you validate a caregiver's feelings with such a statement, she is more likely to feel heard and respected and therefore may be more receptive to your requests or recommendations.

Share your observations in a straightforward, uncritical way. Focus on the child's behaviors and concerns rather than on diagnostic labels. Keep in mind that only a mental health expert can make a diagnosis of a disorder. Describing the child's behavior not only provides valuable information but also is a better way to communicate with caregivers about concerns. The following table illustrates some guidelines.

Guideline	Instead of . . .	Try . . .
Instead of making generalizations about a child, give concrete examples of what you are seeing.	Jud can't control himself. He always needs an adult with him.	Today at story time, Jud got up from the circle every few minutes. He settled down when the assistant sat with him and held his hand.
Instead of suggesting a diagnosis, describe the behavior.	I think Diane's got autism.	I've rarely seen Diane interact with any of the children or adults in the classroom. Have you noticed the same thing?
Instead of labeling the child, use descriptive, observational language.	Gabriel seems passive.	I've noticed that when a child takes a toy from Gabriel, he allows it. Then he puts his head down and weeps. He doesn't call for adult help or try to get the toy back. What do you think is going on?
Avoid "always" and "never" statements. Instead, use value-neutral statements such as "I notice," "I've seen," and "It seems that."	Tamara never sits still. She's always running around the room.	I've seen Tamara have a hard time sitting down for activities, even for lunch. At rest time, I notice she often rolls back and forth on her cot and seems to have a hard time settling down. Is she also very active at home?
Frame your concerns as the child lacking life skills rather than being naughty.	Max grabs toys and hits a lot.	Let's think of ways to help Max take turns with the other children.

Explain what you're doing to help the child be successful. Share with a child's caregivers the classroom or child care setting interventions that have worked or not worked, and ask about how things are handled at home. Ask caregivers for their perspective on your observations. Invite caregivers to share their view of the child. Learn from the caregivers' experiences and listen to their suggestions. For example, you might ask, "Do you have any ideas about how I can help Rene settle down for rest?" Ask about the child's behavior at home and whether there have been any changes there, but be tactful and aware of cultural values. Some cultures strongly discourage sharing family information with nonfamily members.

Communicate with families as soon as you have concerns. Establish a working partnership and a sense of trust before the situation gets out of control. Keep lines of communication open while you explore whether the behavior meets the three basic criteria for diagnosing a disorder: the symptoms occur often and last a long time, the symptoms are present in more than one setting, and the symptoms cause significant distress and/or impairment in functioning. Keep the family updated so that your suggestion to have their child screened or referred doesn't come as a complete surprise.

Continue to share positive news. Caregivers need to know that you can see the good in their child and that their child is appreciated as a unique individual. Help everyone keep a balanced perspective on the child.

Suggest getting professional help when needed. Even though you can make changes in the environment or in relationships to support children with social and emotional challenges, sometimes you'll find it necessary and in the child's best interest to refer the child and his family for additional screening and support. Outside professional support might help both the family and the child during stressful times. Qualified mental health professionals have the skills to uncover underlying problems and can help design useful intervention strategies. Be tactful with caregivers when approaching the topic of getting professional assistance, and be alert to cultural values regarding mental illness and seeking help from others, even professionals. For many people, no matter what their cultural background, it's very difficult to turn to "strangers" for help, particularly with their children and especially when the threat of mental illness is involved.

Have resources and referrals available for caregivers. Often caregivers don't know where to start in order to get psychological evaluation or treatment for their child. If your setting has a mental health consultant, you can turn to him or her. Otherwise, your local professional association (for example, the local Association for the Education of Young Children or a resources and referral agency) or the state department of health, of education, or of human services may be of help. See Appendix D for additional resources.

OFFERING SUGGESTIONS

Caregivers may ask you for suggestions about managing discipline and guidance challenges at home. Consider sharing some of the following ideas, as well as other techniques and interventions covered in this book, during home visits or during parent education meetings.

Suggest ways caregivers can prevent problems. For example, caregivers might want to give their four-year-old, who wakes up scared at night, a flashlight he can take to bed with him.

Show caregivers how to offer alternatives. This is an especially useful skill when working with two-year-olds. Teach caregivers how to ask questions that offer options, such as "Do you want to wear your red socks or your blue socks?" or "Should we walk to the bathroom or jump to the bathroom?"

Help caregivers understand the value of explaining expectations. Recommend that caregivers explain what they want a child to do rather than tell her what she's doing wrong. For example, instead of saying, "Stop getting out of bed," say, "I want you to stay in bed until it gets light outside."

Talk with caregivers about the importance of being calm and in control. When adults show that they can control their anger, children learn that they too can manage their anger.

Share timelines for typical childhood development. Help families have realistic expectations of children by sharing information on typical development. Refer to Appendix A as a guide.

You may wish to reproduce and hand out to families the following Tips for Families chart, which summarizes some of the healthy caregiving principles from this book.

Tips for Families

HELPING CHILDREN DEVELOP EMOTIONAL AND BEHAVIORAL HEALTH

When you . . .	Children will . . .
Spend time talking, playing, and reading with your child every day	Learn how to give and get love, see you as a role model, and develop a love of life and a desire to learn and grow
Accept your child as a unique person with his or her own temperaments, talents, likes, and dislikes	Feel valued as individuals and learn to respect and appreciate themselves and others, enabling them to develop their own special talents
Teach your child about your family's values and culture	Understand who they are, where they come from, and the roles and values you expect for them
Help your child understand and express feelings	Learn empathy and understand that their feelings are nothing to be afraid or ashamed of, so that they learn how to express their feelings in appropriate ways
Encourage both independence and cooperation	Learn to help themselves and learn how to work with, play with, and help each other

PART

2

Descriptions and
Diagnostic Criteria for
Common Psychological
Disorders

INTRODUCTION

In this section, we'll explore in detail specific mental disorders commonly diagnosed in children.

In chapter 1, we described the criteria for a psychological disorder. We said that a disorder is suspected when the child shows serious deviations from what is expected developmentally and culturally and also exhibits symptoms that meet all of the following criteria. These criteria apply to all of the disorders you will learn about in this section.

- Symptoms occur often and last a long time.

- Symptoms are present in more than one setting.

- Symptoms cause significant distress and/or impairment in functioning.

In chapters 2 and 3, we discussed some important observation and management concepts as well as practices for working effectively with the challenging behaviors children with mental health issues might exhibit. The classroom and child care setting strategies for specific disorders provided in this section assume that your classroom or setting makes use of the concepts and approaches from earlier chapters and that it has a strong foundation for promoting social-emotional development. The specific interventions suggested for each diagnostic category in this section will be much harder to implement and may not be successful if the basic foundation is not there.

Each chapter in this section introduces specific disorders and offers suggestions for responding effectively to children with these disorders. Each disorder description includes a vignette describing a typical child with the disorder. Then the symptoms, causes, and treatments of the disorder are discussed, followed by classroom and child care setting strategies you can use.

Much of the information on symptoms and treatments in the following chapters draws on the expertise of two standard reference books used by child psychologists, psychiatrists, and other professional counselors who diagnose and treat children. The most commonly used book, the *Diagnostic and Statistical Manual of Mental Disorders*, Fourth Edition, Text Revision (DSM-IV-TR), is published by the American Psychiatric Association and presents diagnostic criteria, descriptions, and other information to guide practitioners in classifying and diagnosing mental disorders. *The Diagnostic Classification of Mental Health and Developmental Disorders of Infancy and Early Childhood*, Revised Edition (DC:0–3R) is a more recent reference book. It presents a system for diagnosing mental health and developmental disorders in infants and toddlers, with diagnostic categories that reflect the consensus of a multidisciplinary group of experts in early childhood development and mental health.

Please see the bibliography for additional resources that were consulted to expand on causes and treatments in this section of the book. The classroom and child care strategies have been used personally by this book's authors in their work with challenging children. These strategies are a synthesis of ideas from a wide variety of resources.

As you learn more about the nature of each disorder, how to be on the lookout for symptoms, and how to work together with primary caregivers and mental health professionals for the benefit of the child, you'll gain confidence and skills that will contribute to the child's improved emotional health and social development.

CHAPTER 5: Attachment Disturbances

Not so long ago, unwanted children often were raised in foundling homes where basic needs for things like food and warmth were met but where they had little to no interaction with caregivers beyond elementary care. Many of these children did not live beyond their third year, and those who did suffered from notable developmental delays (Spitz 1946). These disturbing results made it clear that, in order to thrive, children must have stable and loving interactions that foster healthy attachment to primary caregivers.

Healthy attachment is generally considered to be a warm, loving bond between an infant and caregiver that is consistent and predictable over time. The attachment relationship provides many experiences and interactions that are essential for healthy social-emotional development, such as instilling a sense of self-worth and fostering the ability to understand the nature of relationships and the ability to self-regulate or self-soothe.

Developmental research suggests that infants' cognitive capacities are highly advanced (Beebe and Lachmann 2002). Even at birth, they have some sense of cause and effect and can figure out what comes next. If an infant's parent typically picks her up when she cries and attends to her needs, the baby learns "If I call for help, somebody will come." By four months of age, infants can remember events and can sense the mood of their caregivers. With these basic skills, very young children, whose lives are dominated by experiences with their caregivers, learn a great deal from their interactions with caregivers and develop the attachment needed for healthy development.

Early Caregiver Influences on Children: A Review

Early experiences with primary caregivers provide the foundation for many aspects of healthy development.

SELF-ESTEEM AND SELF-EFFICACY

If primary caregivers are responsive and nurturing, children are more likely to sense that they have value and that others can be depended on for support and comfort. They learn that when they communicate their needs to others, their needs will usually be met. When children grow up in an environment where their cries for help, food, or comfort get no response, they come to distrust their ability to get their needs met and they often feel unvalued. Neglect, unrealistic expectations, and harsh or inconsistent caregiving can contribute to feelings of unworthiness, discouragement, and anxiety.

UNDERSTANDING THE NATURE OF HUMAN RELATIONSHIPS

Successful social relationships are important for mental health. A child whose first experiences with relationships are warm, supportive, loving, and positive is more likely to bring this expectation to future relationships. Likewise, children whose first experiences with relationships are negative or hurtful will bring this expectation to future relationships, causing them to be wary, protective, and slow to trust. A child with negative relationship experiences will likely have limited knowledge about how to interact appropriately and positively with others, resulting in poor social skills.

UNDERSTANDING THE NATURE OF THE WORLD

A child raised by a loving, attentive caregiver is more likely to develop a sense of the world as a kind and gentle place. A child raised by a neglectful, harsh, or inconsistent caregiver will likely develop a sense that the world is a cold, unloving, and hurtful place without much hope for closeness and contentment.

SELF-REGULATION

The primary caregiver acts as a "co-regulator" to infants, who enter the world with little ability to regulate their behaviors and responses for themselves. A primary caregiver who provides routines, consistent expectations, appropriate soothing experiences, and support in managing distress will help a child internalize her ability to self-soothe and self-regulate. A primary caregiver who leaves the child feeling confused and uncertain about what comes next and how to handle his natural frustration and distress leaves him vulnerable to difficulties with self-regulation. Some researchers believe that basic difficulties with self-regulation can lead to the significantly increased likelihood of developing mental disorders later in childhood (Schore 1999).

EFFECTS ON BRAIN DEVELOPMENT

According to some studies, early caregiving experiences affect brain development, creating expectations and ways of interacting that become harder and harder to change over time. If attachment difficulties are not identified early on, the child is likely to have significant social or emotional challenges. Poor attachment also can result in developmental delays in other areas, such as language and motor skills. This is particularly true for children whose caregivers are neglectful and do not give them enough opportunities to interact and move around.

Healthy Attachment

GENERAL STAGES OF HEALTHY SOCIAL DEVELOPMENT AND ATTACHMENT*

Age	Child
0–3 months	• turns toward familiar voices • smiles in response to a smile • takes turns making noises • begins to display emotions such as happiness and sadness (not just distress)
3–6 months	• begins to show a preference for familiar people • engages in more turn-taking games such as peek-a-boo • begins to display more types of emotions, including anger
7–12 months	• begins to show a strong preference for primary caregivers (this is called *focused attachment*) • becomes aware of emotions in other people • begins to develop "object permanence" or the ability to keep an image of someone or something in mind even when that person or thing is not present • can move and explore the environment • develops normal separation and stranger anxiety
12–18 months	• begins to walk and talk, leading to increased independence through communication and exploration • frequently imitates words, gestures, and movements • develops more independent behavior, but needs the primary caregiver to remain nearby (this is called the *secure base phenomenon*) • continues to have separation and stranger anxiety • has an interest in peers and in parallel (side-by-side) play • begins to develop pretend or symbolic play (e.g., pretending to eat or to sleep)

* The information in this chart is compiled from three sources (Linder 1993; Crockenberg and Leerkes 2000; Marvin and Britner 1999).

Age	Child
18–36 months	• develops a big increase in language abilities • is able to remember past experiences and sequences of events • can tell others about experiences • is able to recognize himself in pictures and mirrors • is able to evaluate herself (e.g., "I was or was not able to accomplish something" and "good versus bad") • becomes self-conscious and is able to notice feelings of shame, guilt, and embarrassment • begins to develop empathy for others • can make decisions based on others' needs and expectations • develops interactive play with peers and dramatic play skills • some children between the ages of 24 and 48 months show an increase in aggressive behavior
3–5 years	• experiences reduced separation and stranger anxiety • enjoys cooperative play with peers • has a strong sense of self, family, and home • prefers challenging tasks • begins social problem-solving • begins to use feeling words appropriately • can self-soothe

Even the most loving, nurturing caregivers make mistakes or are not at their best all the time. Most children can weather the typical ups and downs of occasional imperfect parenting. In fact, if a caring parent makes a mistake or is unable to meet a need, the child can often experience a sense of hope and expectation of working things out with caregivers when the situation is fixed or addressed. This can be part of a healthy attachment relationship.

Attachment Problems and Reactive Attachment Disorder Symptoms at a Glance

- hard to engage socially or often "shuts down"
- jumpy or easily startled
- rejects attempts of others to provide love and comforting
- exhibits aggression
- engages in solitary play
- shows oppositional behavior
- is overly friendly with strangers
- exhibits needy, clingy behavior
- exhibits inappropriate touching
- becomes very upset when people come and go

Other difficulties or characteristics that resemble attachment problems or reactive attachment disorder include the following:

- posttraumatic stress disorder (PTSD)
- separation anxiety disorder
- oppositional defiant disorder
- attention-deficit/hyperactivity disorder
- depression
- bipolar disorder
- regulatory disorder
- pervasive developmental disorders such as autism
- mental retardation

Attachment Problems and Reactive Attachment Disorder

In the toddler room, Maritza runs over to a new aide she's never met before and hugs her legs hard. She takes the aide's hand and leads her over to the soft chairs, sits on her lap, and wants to be read to. The aide is surprised but also a little flattered by all this attention. While sitting on her lap, Maritza begins playing with the aide's hair, kissing her hands over and over, and snuggling deeply into her body. When the aide gets up to leave, Maritza begs her not to go. Maritza throws herself on the floor and cries, as she often does when anyone leaves the room.

LeRoy is extremely shut down. When someone tries to talk or play with him, he moves away or turns his back. He doesn't try to engage with anyone and doesn't seem to notice when other people come and go, even those he has known for a long time. He pays no attention when his mother leaves in the morning and hardly looks up when she comes in to get him in the afternoon. Because he's so resistant to engaging, it's hard to get him to follow classroom routines and rules. He often melts down and gets angry and aggressive. The rest of the time he shows few emotions and has little interest in others.

TYPICAL SYMPTOMS

Children with severe attachment problems may be diagnosed with reactive attachment disorder (RAD), which is most common among children who have been raised in institutions or who have been adopted internationally. Although you may sometimes have in your classroom or setting children with a full RAD diagnosis, you're more likely to have children who have attachment difficulties somewhere along the spectrum from mild to severe. Children who do not meet all the RAD criteria may still require intervention and treatment.

Here is a summary of the symptoms of RAD (adapted from the DSM-IV-TR) that must occur before age five:

- There is evidence of significant abuse or neglect. The child's basic physical needs and his ongoing need for affection and love have not been met. For some children, multiple changes in primary caregivers may have prevented the formation of an adequate attachment relationship.

- The child doesn't initiate or respond to social interactions in ways typical of a child her age. With one type of RAD, a child might seem "shut down" and difficult to engage. She may be jumpy and startle easily, or she may seem confused about attachment interactions. For example, she might seem to want to go to her caregiver but then avoids eye contact, or she might push her caregiver away when the caregiver tries to comfort her.

- With another type of RAD, a child may be overly friendly and intimate with an adult he barely knows and may fall apart when that person tries to leave the area. This behavior is called *indiscriminate sociability*. This behavior is often mistaken as a sign that the child is friendly and happy, but this degree of overly social behavior is not a healthy sign.

CAUSES

Attachment disturbances typically result from a problem in the child's primary attachment relationship. This can occur for several reasons:

- The unexpected loss of a primary caregiver (for example, through death, imprisonment, or abandonment)

- A caregiver who is not consistently available (for example, when a caregiver is depressed or has a mental illness)

- Intrusive or angry caregiving (for example, when a caregiver is stressed and feeling overwhelmed with the demands of a baby)

- Abusive and/or neglectful caregiving

- Repeated changes in caregivers, either in foster care or when a child is moved frequently within a family (for example, when a parent drops the child off at different relatives' houses for months at a time)

TREATMENT

Therapy for RAD and attachment problems often focuses on the relationship between the child and the caregiver. Often, the caregiver was also raised in an abusive or neglectful family. A caregiver who was raised in a nonsupportive and loveless environment may not be able to provide support and love for her own child. She often needs to be given information about the basic social-emotional needs of her child and how she can meet those needs. She may need individual mental health treatment and support as well. She also needs sensitivity and support from her child's providers. Relate to the caregiver in a way that models how you'd like her to relate to her child. Sometimes caregivers need help with basic needs, such as housing, food, and transportation. Providing a child with emotional support can be especially challenging for the caregiver when basic family needs are unmet.

When children with RAD are adopted, the new primary caregivers have the responsibility to work on attaching to the child and providing predictable and positive social interactions. Children with RAD often reject adults' attachment attempts. Caregivers need a great deal of patience and support to form attachments with these children, especially if the children are aggressive or have tantrums. Caregivers will need to learn how to be loving and firm at the same time. They will probably benefit from coaching on how to set firm limits and how to guide children without being punitive, threatening, or rejecting.

Interventions that include physical restraint or coercion, such as "holding therapy" and "rebirthing therapy," are not recommended (American Academy of Child and Adolescent Psychiatry 2004). Children with highly aggressive behavior may need medications that reduce aggression. Antidepressants may also be given if the child is persistently depressed or anxious.

CLASSROOM AND CHILD CARE SETTING STRATEGIES

Stay in communication with caregivers. Children improve most when all of their adult caregivers work together as a united team. Children with attachment problems require consistency, and they need to know that all the adults in their life are in constant communication. For help with establishing and maintaining communication with caregivers, refer to the suggestions in chapter 4.

Designate a primary "go to" person for the child. This may be the provider to whom the child seems naturally drawn. The child's "go to" provider should provide most of the interventions and attachment activities and be available as the main comforter.

Create a consistent, predictable schedule. Create routines and rituals around hellos, good-byes, and transitions. Talk to children in advance when there will be a separation or absence. Prepare them for breaks and vacations. Some children need to know if you'll be stepping out of the classroom even for a few moments. Make sure you tell them when you're leaving and when you'll be back. Caregivers should never "sneak out" when the child isn't looking.

Provide attachment activities that include touching, rocking, eye contact, movement, physical closeness, give-and-take interactions, and shared emotion. Here are some examples:

- Peek-a-boo games

- This Little Piggy game

- Lullaby singing while maintaining eye contact

- Combing hair or washing the child's face while commenting on the process. The provider might say, "I'm combing your pretty brown hair. It's so long and beautiful" or "I see your big brown eyes and those long eyelashes on your handsome face."

- Pushing on the swing. Be sure to face the child while you're pushing, and continue to talk about the interaction.

Becky Bailey's book *I Love You Rituals* provides many more ideas for games to help children and adults attach in healthy ways.

For children who are very shut down or not yet ready to engage in attachment play, start simply. Greet the child warmly every day. Sit next to him and talk for a short period of time each day, even if he doesn't respond. Comment on what he's doing. Say, for example, "Oh, I see you're playing with the cars. I like cars too." Another time, ask if you can play, and follow the child's lead in the activity. For example, say, "I like to play cars too. Can I play?" and then sit next to him and move the cars the same way he does. Such joint activity helps the child become comfortable with shared interaction.

Provide the overly needy and indiscriminate child with loving, appropriate, clear limits. You may have to limit the child's social behavior. For example, she may try to touch you inappropriately. Be firm with your limits and calm and supportive in your redirection. For example, say, "No, thank you. I don't like it when you touch me there" or "We don't know Mr. Tom. Let's shake his hand. Hugs are for special people we've known for a long time."

Teach basic social and emotional skills. Help children learn to recognize and verbalize their feelings and needs. Use the active listening techniques described in chapter 3. Provide opportunities for teaching play entry-and-exit skills, either in a group setting or through one-on-one monitoring and support. Free-choice time is an especially good time for learning these skills.

Be aware that the child with attachment difficulties has significant unmet emotional needs. He is not trying to upset you or to make your life difficult, even when he's shut down, aggressive, having a tantrum, or begging for endless attention and affection. You must be patient, warm, firm, and consistent.

CHAPTER 6: Regulatory Disorders

This chapter provides a detailed description of regulatory disorders and how you can help children with these disorders. We'll first explain what self-regulation is and how it develops.

Understanding Self-Regulation

Infants are born helpless and disorganized. They suddenly have to deal with many things that weren't there before they entered the world, including feeling hunger and needing to signal their desire to eat; experiencing wet and dirty diapers; feeling too hot or too cold; and experiencing a need for comfort and closeness. Also new is a vast array of intense sensory experiences. Nothing is familiar and they are unable to predict what will happen next. They need a lot of help to get through their days and nights, and they have few ways to communicate their needs. The foundation of self-regulation is provided by the primary caregiver. A consistent, predictable, loving, and available relationship with a primary caregiver helps infants learn that their needs will be met and what to expect next. They learn how to self-regulate—that is, how to manage emotions, how to soothe themselves, how to learn about the world, and how to manage all the sensory information.

For example, when a caregiver responds to an infant's cue that he's hungry, tired, wet, or in need of being held and cuddled, the infant learns that his needs will be met and that there is somebody he can count on. Daily rituals and routines help him learn what to expect next. He starts to understand how the world works and that it is predictable. Without these experiences, an infant is likely to feel that the world is chaotic and overwhelming, which is likely to make it harder for him to manage his behavior and distress.

Caregivers also teach children ways to manage emotions. When a baby is upset, the caregiver may hold her, rock her, or sing to her. Such soothing is called co-regulation. When the caregiver co-regulates, she is teaching the baby that there are ways to calm down or to be soothed. When a caregiver does not bond with the baby, is inconsistent or harsh, or does not help to soothe the baby when she's distressed, the infant doesn't have the opportunity to experience ways to calm herself and feel better. She may also feel unimportant and very alone in the world. Such a baby will not have the basic foundation she needs to learn how to manage her emotions.

Caregivers also help infants learn about their senses. As a caregiver plays with and takes care of a baby, the infant is exposed to many sights and sounds. Babies learn about movement from rocking and going for walks. Babies learn about touch from bathing and diapering. Singing and talking teaches a baby about sounds and language. These early experiences help a baby start to learn how to process and organize sensory input.

Starting right from their birth, some children seem fussier and more irritable than others. Caregivers may tell you that their baby had colic and cried on and on for no reason. They may tell you that nothing they did seemed to help much. Fortunately, colicky behavior seems to fade out by about six months of age. Other children just seem to have what we commonly call a difficult temperament. They are more easily upset by little things and need more help to calm down and to relax. Both colic and a difficult temperament can be a part of typical development.

Children with regulatory disorders have difficulty organizing and regulating many different types of experiences, including eating and sleeping and their attention spans, emotions, and sensory experiences. Regulatory disorders are a relatively new diagnostic category. More research needs to be done to shed further light on them.

Regulatory Disorder Symptoms at a Glance

Hypersensitive	Hyposensitive/ underresponsive	Sensory stimulation- seeking/impulsive
• overly sensitive to normal sensory stimulation • avoids stimulation • cries or has tantrums when overstimulated • hard to soothe • irritable/aggressive • withdrawn	• unresponsive • hard to engage • slow moving • likes repetitive play • poor body awareness • likes intense stimula- tion such as jumping or deep hugs	• very active • takes physical risks • impulsive • always seeks physical contact • poor attention • easily excited • aggressive

These signs and symptoms can occur for short periods in any child, so, with regulatory disorders, it's especially important to remember that a diagnosable disorder is suspected when the child shows the following:

- serious deviations from what is expected developmentally and culturally

- symptoms that occur often and last a long time

- symptoms that are present in more than one setting

- symptoms that cause significant distress and/or impairment in functioning

Other difficulties or characteristics that might resemble regulatory disorders include the following:

- problems in the primary attachment relationship

- aggression, poor attention, or withdrawal secondary to other delays, such as language development or other learning disorders

- pervasive developmental disorders, such as autism

- attention-deficit/hyperactivity disorder

- oppositional defiant disorder

- depression or anxiety disorders, including posttraumatic stress disorder

- bipolar disorder

Regulatory Disorders

Three-year-old Raymond recently joined a classroom. Most of the time he seems scared or nervous. He refuses to do certain types of activities. He tends to crawl under the table with his favorite toy during choice time. He hates having his hands washed and will not touch or eat any foods that are soft or slimy. If other kids accidentally brush against him, he tries to wipe away the spot and then gets upset and cries. He doesn't explore the classroom or new toys the way the other children do. He's fussy a lot, but it's hard to tell what sets him off. Often his distress turns into a tantrum. He seems to get more upset if the provider tries to touch him or distract him with toys or activities. Raymond calms down best when he can get to a quiet, soothing area away from others. Naptimes are very difficult for him. He often lies awake wiggling around for a long time.

TYPICAL SYMPTOMS

The DSM-IV-TR doesn't include regulatory disorders as a formal diagnosis for children. The DC:0–3R has established criteria for three different types of regulatory disorders:

- hypersensitive

- hyposensitive/underresponsive

- sensory stimulation-seeking/impulsive

The DC:0–3R criteria emphasize the role of sensory processing in the diagnosis of regulatory disorders. *Sensory processing* is making sense of information coming from one or more of the five senses (seeing, hearing, touching, smelling, and tasting). To receive a diagnosis of a regulatory disorder, a child must have both a sensory processing problem and a regulatory problem in another area, such as with attention span or emotion. Mental health professionals sometimes use the terms *sensory processing disorder* and *sensory integration dysfunction* when talking about a regulatory disorder. These terms are specific to problems with sensory processing. According to some clinicians and researchers, a child may have a sensory processing disorder without having difficulties in other areas of regulation, although this experience is relatively rare (DeGangi 2000).

Hypersensitive Regulatory Disorder

Children with a hypersensitive regulatory disorder are more sensitive to sensory input than most people are. Everyday experiences can feel overwhelming to them.

TYPICAL SYMPTOMS

According to the DC:0–3R, there are two kinds of hypersensitivity in children. Some children react by being fearful or cautious (Type A, or fearful/cautious). Other children react with negative or defiant behaviors (Type B, or negative/defiant). Children who are fearful/cautious have the following symptoms (adapted from the DC:0–3R):

- Hypersensitivity (being overly sensitive) to sensory stimulation. When exposed to sensory stimulation, they startle easily, feel afraid, cry a lot, and may even have tantrums. They may freeze or try to get away. They get distracted easily and might even become aggressive.

- Physical deficits connected to a lack of experience with exploring the environment. Children may struggle with fine motor skills such as stringing beads or balancing blocks. They may have poor posture and look a bit "floppy." They tend to be clumsy, drop things, and bump into people without realizing it. They may avoid playing with toys that are overly stimulating, such as toys with flashing lights or unusual textures.

- Additional behavioral problems, including a lack of interest in exploration, a lack of assertiveness, distress at changes in routines, fear of new situations, an unusual number of fears or worries, shyness, impulsivity and distractibility, irritability, limited ability to self-soothe, and difficulty recovering from frustration or disappointment.

Children who are negative/defiant will have the same symptoms, but they will also be much more irritable, fussy, angry, controlling, and defiant. They also tend to have more frequent tantrums.

CAUSES

Little research has been done about the causes of regulatory disorders. Some evidence shows that such disorders might be hereditary. Other studies connect the disorders to problems during pregnancy and childbirth, such as a mother's drug use or exposure to toxins. Complications during pregnancy or delivery and premature birth also may affect a child's ability to regulate. Long hospital stays or being institutionalized can have negative effects on self-regulation (Kranowitz 1998). Neglect, harsh interactions, and abuse may also diminish a child's ability to develop appropriate self-regulation skills.

TREATMENT

Children with regulatory disorders need help from a team of professionals and caregivers. Occupational and physical therapists usually design for the child a plan called a "sensory diet," which is based on the child's individual needs. The diet usually includes fun activities that give the child practice responding appropriately to the kinds of sensory experiences that normally give him problems. For example, the child may be given objects with different textures to explore, the therapist might use a brush to stroke the child's skin, or the therapist might play games with the child that include shouting and whispering. These games and activities help the child learn to take in and respond to sensory input and to complete basic self-help activities comfortably.

As always, primary and secondary caregivers need to be involved in helping the child. Therapists help families understand what the child is experiencing. They teach primary caregivers how to help the child at home and teach providers how to help in the child care setting or classroom. Therapists may make suggestions about how to change the environment by adding or decreasing stimulation, depending on the child's needs. They may help caregivers develop ways of providing additional learning experiences that promote emotional and attentional regulation. Therapists may also help caregivers with behavioral plans and discipline skills that work best for children with sensory challenges. Medication may be used to treat severe behavior problems such as aggression, tantrums, and recklessness.

CLASSROOM AND CHILD CARE SETTING STRATEGIES

Stay in communication with caregivers. Children improve most when all of their adult caregivers work together as a united team. Children with hypersensitivity require consistency, and they need to know that all the adults in their life are in regular communication. For suggestions about establishing and maintaining communication with caregivers see chapter 4.

Observe and identify triggers. Each child who is hypersensitive is unique. Some are more sensitive to sight, others to sound. A child may be sensitive to more than one sensory experience. Observe the child to identify what kinds of sensory experiences trigger her distress. As you observe, take note of when the trouble happens. Does it occur all day long, every time there's a loud noise or flashing light? Or does the child seem fine early in the day but more sensitive as the day moves on? Sometimes sensory overstimulation can be cumulative. The child may start the day in a good mood and be able to tolerate certain sensory input. Later in the day, when she's reached the limit of how much sensory input she can tolerate in a day, she may have an intense meltdown over something relatively small. Information you gather from observing the child will help you come up with the best plan for meeting her individual needs.

Minimize triggers that create intense distress. If a child gets distressed in large group activities with a lot of movement and noise, offer an alternative small-group or one-on-one activity at the same time. If a child has a tantrum every time another child takes his toy, have more than one of his favorite toys available. If a child becomes aggressive when touched lightly or brushed against, give him deep hugs and strong pats. Don't, however, shy away from making developmentally appropriate demands on the child. Help him take part in routines, with modifications. For example, let him sit in a beanbag chair during circle time if that helps him stay calm, or let him hold your hand as you walk through a busy, noisy area together.

Stick to a predictable routine. And schedule "sensory breaks" if the child seems to show the cumulative effect of too much sensory input.

Evaluate and adjust the environment. Children who are very sensitive need an environment with limited stimulation. Keep materials and supplies tidy and contained. Close shelves and bins that are not being used. Organize wall displays to avoid excess and clutter. Avoid playing music as background noise during center time.

Establish a calm place in the room where the child can go when she's feeling overwhelmed. This area should have very little stimulation. One idea is to put soft pillows and a few cuddly toys in a corner screened off with netting. Invite children to use this area when they are getting upset.

Give a warning before you start a transition process. Overly sensitive children may struggle with transitions and changes in routines and will stay calmer if they know in advance what to expect. Talk about what is going to happen and how it will be different.

Promote a healthy sensory diet. Good examples of sensory activities are fingerpainting, sampling fruits at a fruit-tasting table, or searching for buried items in a tub filled with sand. Activities like these provide sensory experiences in a controlled way. Vary the activities to maintain interest. Encourage the child to join by offering choices: "Would you like to fingerpaint or play in the sand table this morning?"

Offer activities that provide pleasant sensory experiences throughout the day. Some options are rocking in a chair, swinging on a swing, rubbing or patting backs at rest time, or swaddling young infants.

Help the child develop self-soothing skills. Show the child how to snuggle with a soft toy. Give him a transitional object to help him move from place to place. For example, you might let the child be the one to carry the signal bell you use when the class goes outdoors and returns indoors. Teach the child how to calm himself by hugging his hands against his chest or by listening to music or looking at a book.

Hyposensitive/Underresponsive Regulatory Disorder

Hyposensitive or underresponsive children are less sensitive to sensory input than most people are and can often seem hard to reach.

TYPICAL SYMPTOMS

Children who are hyposensitive/underresponsive typically have the following symptoms (adapted from the DC:0–3R):

- Underreactive to sensory stimulation. They don't seem to notice sights, sounds, touch, smell, taste, and movement the way other children the same age do. They may have difficulty with proprioception (the ability to know where their body is in space). They also don't notice when others greet them or invite them to play.

- Tendency to be tired and slow moving. They don't explore the environment much and prefer to play with the same things over and over. They may be clumsy, because they don't notice things and don't know where their body is in space. At times, in order to feel connected, they will try to seek out specific sensory input—such as jumping or swinging—over and over.

- Lack of interest in and attention for exploring, playing games, and interacting with others. These experiences don't seem to provide the child with enough stimulation. In order to be engaged, underreactive children need a lot more input than other children do.

CAUSES

As with hypersensitivity disorder, little research has been done about the causes of regulatory disorders. Some evidence shows that such disorders might be hereditary. Other studies connect the disorders to problems during pregnancy and childbirth, such as a mother's drug use or exposure to toxins. Complications during pregnancy or delivery and premature birth also may affect a child's ability to regulate. Long hospital stays or being institutionalized can have negative effects on self-regulation (Kranowitz 1998). Neglect, harsh interactions, and abuse may also diminish a child's ability to develop appropriate self-regulation skills.

TREATMENT

Children with regulatory disorders need help from a team of professionals and caregivers. Occupational and physical therapists usually design for the child a plan called a "sensory diet," which is based on the child's individual needs. The diet usually includes fun activities that give the child practice responding appropriately to the kinds of sensory experiences that normally give him problems. For example, the child may be given objects with different textures to explore, the therapist might use a brush to stroke the child's skin, or the therapist might play games with the child that include shouting and whispering. These games and activities help the child learn to take in and respond to sensory input and to complete basic self-help activities comfortably.

As always, primary and secondary caregivers need to be involved in helping the child. Therapists help families understand what the child is experiencing. They teach primary caregivers how to help the child at home and teach providers how to help in the child care setting or classroom. Therapists may make suggestions about how to change the environment by adding or decreasing stimulation, depending on the child's needs. They may help caregivers develop ways of providing additional learning experiences that promote emotional and attentional regulation. Therapists may also help caregivers with behavioral plans and discipline skills that work best for children with sensory challenges. Medication may be used to treat severe behavior problems such as aggression, tantrums, and recklessness.

CLASSROOM AND CHILD CARE SETTING STRATEGIES

Stay in communication with caregivers. Children improve most when all of their adult caregivers work together as a united team. Children who are hyposensitive/underresponsive require consistency, and they need to know that all the adults in their life are in regular communication. For suggestions about establishing and maintaining communication with caregivers, see chapter 4.

Encourage the child to interact with others. Motivate the child to participate by offering activities with strong sensory input. Examples include gross motor activities, such as running, jumping, completing obstacle courses, or pushing or pulling heavy objects.

Remember that underresponsive children may need extra time to respond. Be patient. Look for subtle, nonverbal responses as well.

Encourage interaction by following the child's lead in play, even when it is slow and limited. Talk out loud about the play and what is happening. During the play, model social responses and emotions. For example, you might say, "Can I have a turn at the hose now?" or "This is so much fun building a tower with you."

Provide underresponsive children with the extra stimulation they need to become alert and involved. Once involved, they can become overstimulated easily, so as they begin responding, slow down or lessen the activity as needed.

Sensory Stimulation-Seeking/Impulsive Regulatory Disorder

Children with sensory stimulation-seeking/impulsive regulatory disorder are driven to find sensory experiences. Because they love a lot of stimulation, they are sensation seekers and sometimes do dangerous things such as climbing on top of a toy shelf or jumping off the swing. They are very active and, because they take risks, may have many accidents.

TYPICAL SYMPTOMS *(adapted from the DC:0–3R)*

- Appear hyperactive and are on the go all the time. Can be impulsive and have a lot of accidents without appearing clumsy.

- Seek a lot of physical contact. They often touch other children, hug hard, and like to wrestle. At rest time, they may like having their backs rubbed or patted very hard, or they may want to be rocked fast on the rocking chair.

- Appear aimless and unorganized when they're not immediately engaged in an activity that offers them some stimulation.

- Exhibit additional behavioral problems, including getting easily excited and out of control, being physically aggressive, and barging into the play and conversation of others.

CAUSES

As with hypersensitivity disorder, little research has been done about the causes of regulatory disorders. Some evidence shows that such disorders might be hereditary. Other studies connect the disorders to problems during pregnancy and childbirth, such as a mother's drug use or exposure to toxins. Complications during pregnancy or delivery and premature birth also may affect a child's ability to regulate. Long hospital stays or being institutionalized can have negative effects on self-regulation (Kranowitz 1998). Neglect, harsh interactions, and abuse may also diminish a child's ability to develop appropriate self-regulation skills.

TREATMENT

Children with regulatory disorders need help from a team of professionals and caregivers. Occupational and physical therapists usually design for the child a plan called a "sensory diet," which is based on the child's individual needs. The diet usually includes fun activities that give the child practice responding appropriately to the kinds of sensory experiences that normally give him problems. For example, the child may be given objects with different textures to explore, the therapist might use a brush to stroke the child's skin, or the therapist might play games with the child that include shouting and whispering. These games and activities help the child learn to take in and respond to sensory input and to complete basic self-help activities comfortably.

As always, primary and secondary caregivers need to be involved in helping the child. Therapists help families understand what the child is experiencing. They teach primary caregivers how to help the child at home and teach providers how to help in the child care setting or classroom. Therapists may make suggestions about how to change the environment by adding or decreasing stimulation, depending on the child's needs. They may help caregivers develop ways of providing additional learning experiences that promote emotional and attentional regulation. Therapists may also help caregivers with behavioral plans and discipline skills that work best for children with sensory challenges. Medication may be used to treat severe behavior problems such as aggression, tantrums, and recklessness.

CLASSROOM AND CHILD CARE SETTING STRATEGIES

Stay in communication with caregivers. Children improve most when all of their adult caregivers work together as a united team. Children who are sensation seekers require consistency, and they need to know that all the adults in their life are in regular communication. For suggestions about establishing and maintaining communication with caregivers, see chapter 4.

Provide developmentally appropriate activities that offer children stimulation. Offer a balance of large motor (gross motor) and small motor (fine motor) activities, such as fingerpainting; water play; marching; pushing, pulling, or carrying heavy objects; jumping and running; and obstacle courses.

Use firm touch. Sensation-seeking children respond well to firm touch. Deep-pressure rubbing on a child's back during naptime can help ease the transition to sleep. Rubbing lotion on her arms or using heavy patting on her back can also help.

Allow the child *some* kind of sensory stimulation during activities that require sitting still and paying attention. During circle time, the sensory-seeking child may do better if he's allowed to sit on a beanbag chair or to squeeze a ball.

Be patient. Remember that the child is not purposely trying to annoy you or disrupt the classroom or setting. She's using limited skills to try to organize herself and her interactions in response to circumstances that seem overwhelming to her.

Provide extra supervision. Because these children are often risk takers and thrill seekers, they need more oversight than other children do. Patiently redirect them to safer and more appropriate activities when they are in danger of getting hurt. For example, guide a child to climb the monkey bars instead of the fence. If he tries to push a bookshelf across the floor, give him a crate with a pulling rope as an alternative.

Provide opportunities to develop self-soothing skills. Try rhythmic activities such as swinging and rocking. Plan large group activities that give children practice with self-regulation in a fun way. Introduce such games as "freeze" and "red light, green light." Include activities that require moving back and forth from gross motor skills to fine motor skills. For example, set up an obstacle course so the children have to run fast, put a peg in a hole, run fast again, and then put a bead on a string. Play games that involve changing tempo, such as rolling the ball fast, then rolling it slowly. Practice singing songs that include singing loudly and then singing softly. For younger children, "I'm gonna getcha" and "tickle monster" games can be beneficial.

CHAPTER 7: Anxiety Disorders

Anxiety disorders involve intense feelings of anxiety, dread, fear, tension, or worry. Some anxiety is normal for babies, toddlers, and preschoolers. For example, separation anxiety is fear or worry when being separated from, or left by, a primary caregiver. Stranger anxiety is fear or worry around unknown persons. Both separation anxiety and stranger anxiety usually develop between seven and twelve months of age. These anxieties gradually fade away by the time a toddler is two-and-a-half years old. Some children experience anxiety when participating in groups because they are temperamentally shy or withdrawn; they may need encouragement and support to try new activities or to join large groups. Cultural influences may also be at play when children exhibit hesitant behavior. In some cultures, girls are expected to be quiet and submissive. Some cultures value a close-knit family that encourages dependence and closeness. In other cultures, children are expected to be independent and self-sufficient. All these factors must be taken into account when observing a child for signs of anxiety.

In this chapter, you'll learn about the three common anxiety disorders diagnosed in young children: posttraumatic stress disorder, separation anxiety disorder, and generalized anxiety disorder. There are other anxiety disorders that are not discussed in this chapter. Two of them, obsessive-compulsive disorder and phobias, are briefly described below.

Anxiety Symptoms at a Glance

Posttraumatic stress disorder (PTSD)	Separation anxiety disorder (SAD)	Generalized anxiety disorder (GAD)
• trauma event • has nightmares/sleep problems • talks about trauma a lot • withdraws • startles easily • loses skills • is aggressive	• struggles against separation from caregiver • cannot be soothed after caregiver leaves • follows caregiver around all the time • is clingy • has nightmares	• worries all the time • needs a lot of reassurance • has difficulty sitting still; is easily distracted • is irritable

Other difficulties that might resemble anxiety disorders include the following:

- problems in the primary attachment relationship

- anxiety secondary to other delays, such as language development or other learning disorders

- attention-deficit/hyperactivity disorder (ADHD)

Obsessive-compulsive disorder (OCD) is rare in very young children. People with OCD have a combination of obsessive thoughts and compulsive behaviors. *Obsessions* are uncontrollable, often irrational thoughts that occur again and again and that cause fear or anxiety. Two examples of obsessions are a fear of being contaminated by germs and constant worrying about whether you've locked the door or turned off the stove. *Compulsions* are repetitive behaviors that may help calm anxiety. For example, someone with an obsession about germs might compulsively wash her hands dozens of times a day. A person obsessed with thoughts about leaving the door unlocked might compulsively go back to check it again and again.

Sometimes the repetitive and rigid behaviors seen in a child with autism resemble symptoms of obsessive-compulsive disorder. A full clinical evaluation with a mental health professional can help to clarify such a concern.

Phobias are unrealistic fears. A phobia can be the fear of a specific thing, such as the fear of dogs or the fear of elevators, or it can be more general, such as the fear of being in social situations (known as a *social phobia*). Because children normally have some fears—of monsters, of the dark, or of dogs, for example—the three criteria for a disorder must also be evident before a phobia diagnosis is made. These three criteria, discussed earlier, are:

- the symptoms occur often and last a long time

- the symptoms are present in more than one setting

- the symptoms cause significant distress and/or impairment in functioning

Posttraumatic Stress Disorder (PTSD)

When her aunt dropped three-year-old Maria off at school one morning, she told the provider that Maria's parents got into a fight the previous night. The police had been called and Maria's dad was taken away to face charges. Her mom had to go to the hospital for stitches. Over the next few weeks, the provider notices some significant changes in Maria: She has a lot of trouble separating from her mom every morning. During the day, instead of playing with the other children, she stays by the side of her favorite provider. She often talks about her dad hurting her mom with a knife, and she asks the provider what happens when people go to the police station. During free time, Maria spends a lot of time at the dollhouse by herself. When the provider walks by one morning, he overhears that the dad doll has a knife and is going to cut the mom. Maria's face is blank during this play. She repeats this same play behavior over and over. On the playground, the provider is surprised to see Maria pushing younger kids, and he has to go over and intervene several times. Maria has difficulty falling asleep at naptime. She freezes and stares when she hears a sudden, unexpected noise. She seems babylike at times and whines and cries for extra help with getting her shoes on and going to the bathroom.

The next time Maria's mother comes to pick her up, the provider learns that Maria is having nightmares and is having difficulty sleeping at home too.

Her mother says that Maria becomes very upset anytime she sees a knife or whenever people argue in front of her. She also says that she doesn't know when her husband might show up at the house again. She is worried about Maria and is also very scared and overwhelmed herself.

TYPICAL SYMPTOMS

To be diagnosed with PTSD, a child must have experienced or witnessed a real or seemingly life-threatening trauma. The trauma can be sudden and unexpected, or it can be chronic or ongoing over a long period of time. Obvious traumatic events include things such as car accidents, natural disasters, and violent crimes. Physical and sexual abuse also can seem life-threatening to a young child, as can domestic violence. Some research has shown that children who *witness* domestic violence are more likely to develop full-blown PTSD than are children who have themselves been victims of direct assault (Scheeringa and Zeanah 1995).

Very young children may experience chronic separation, neglect, and extremely poor caregiving or attachment relationships as trauma. They may feel the lack of an appropriate caregiving relationship as a threat to their ability to survive in the world. This type of trauma is called "relational trauma" (Perry et al. 1995; Schore 2001). To date, little research has been done regarding relational trauma and the development of PTSD. Many children in this category may be identified as having attachment difficulties or are diagnosed with deprivation/maltreatment disorder (Zero to Three 2005).

The DSM-IV-TR diagnostic criteria for diagnosing PTSD focus on adult symptoms, which can be difficult to apply to young children. Until recently, mental health experts thought that young children escaped the effects of trauma because they were unlikely to understand or remember it. However, recent research in early trauma, brain development, and long-term outcomes has shown that very young children can be affected by trauma, even if they cannot remember or talk about the specific event.

The criteria presented here are adapted from the DC:0–3R. To be diagnosed with PTSD, the child must have been exposed to a traumatic event and must exhibit all three of the following symptoms for at least one month:

1. The child reexperiences the trauma in at least one of the following ways:

- The child uses play to reenact the traumatic event. He may replay just one detail, such as yelling, "You bad boy." Or he may replay a whole sequence, such as throwing a baby doll on the bed and hitting the doll while yelling, "You bad boy." Such scenarios differ from creative dramatic play in that the child repeats the same script again and again without change. The child's anxiety does not usually lessen after replaying the scene.

- The child continues to bring up the event. She may tell bits of the story at circle time or at lunch or while playing outside. She may ask many questions about what happened. She may have trouble participating in daily routines without thinking about the event, but she may not seem upset when she talks about it.

- The child has frequent nightmares. These nightmares might recall aspects of the event or they might be totally unrelated.

- The child may get physically distressed when he's reminded of the trauma. His heart might pound hard; he may get an upset stomach or shake and have trouble breathing. Older children might talk about these symptoms, or adults might notice the child having a physical reaction.

- The child has flashbacks about the trauma or has periods of "spacing out." When the child has a flashback, she actually feels that she is back at the scene of the trauma. For the child, this isn't merely a memory. She actually experiences herself as being back in that time and at that place. She may thrash about, screaming, "Stop hurting me, stop hurting me," even though she is totally alone in the home living area. If someone goes over to soothe her, she doesn't see or hear the person. A child also might have periods of "spacing out," in which she "freezes" or stares out into space—this is called "dissociation." A child who is dissociating is not in the here and now and may not respond to a provider's voice or touch at first.

2. The child withdraws from the world and pulls into himself in at least one of the following ways:

- interacts less and less with others

- shows few emotions

- shows less interest in the normal daily routines of life

- avoids activities, places, and people that remind him of the trauma

3. The child seems tense and on edge in at least two of the following ways:

- has sleep problems (refuses to go to sleep, or has trouble falling asleep or staying asleep)

- is easy distracted

- is highly aware of small changes in the environment, such as noises or the movements of others—this is called *hypervigilance*

- startles easily and has a strong response to surprises in the environment, such as noises or someone walking behind her

- is more irritable or fussy and may have outbursts of anger or tantrums

Although the following criteria are not included in the DC:0–3R, children who experience a traumatic event are also likely to

- temporarily lose previously acquired skills—for example, they may wet their pants, suck their thumbs, or say they can't get dressed by themselves, even though they've already passed through these stages;

- be more aggressive—they may hit, push, grab, bite, and disregard the welfare of their playmates;

- be afraid of things they didn't fear before—they may worry about being left alone, be afraid of the dark, and have trouble separating from their caregivers and going to school.

CAUSES

PTSD can be diagnosed only if the child has experienced a life-threatening event or witnessed such an event happening to someone else. No one knows why some children develop PTSD after experiencing a trauma and others do not, although children with a family history of PTSD and depression may be more vulnerable.

TREATMENT

The way to help a child with PTSD varies, depending on what kind of trauma the child experienced. For example, helping a child who experienced a hurricane will be different from helping a child who is experiencing ongoing sexual abuse.

Most often, therapy will include both the child and his family. Families need information about what PTSD is and how it shows up in young children. They need help seeing PTSD behaviors as reactions to trauma and not "naughty" behaviors. Primary caregivers who have been traumatized by the same event may need intervention themselves. Caregivers also need to feel confident about their parenting skills at these times and may need help with behavior management. They need to learn ways to support their children at home, such as how to soothe their child.

Here are some basic principles for treatment of PTSD in children (Scheeringa and Gaensbauer 2000):

- Help the child feel safe and secure.

- Help the child manage strong emotions.

- In terms she can understand, help the child understand the reality of what happened.

- Help the child regain a sense of control.

- Strive to understand and address other emotional and behavioral challenges resulting from the experience.

Medication may be used to help control intense symptoms of anxiety or depression or other behavioral problems that result from PTSD.

CLASSROOM AND CHILD CARE SETTING STRATEGIES

Stay in communication with caregivers. Children improve most when all of their adult caregivers work together as a united team. Children who have experienced trauma require consistency, and they need to know that all the adults in their life are in constant communication. For suggestions about establishing and maintaining communication with caregivers, see chapter 4.

Help the child feel safe. Try not to expose the child to reminders of the trauma. Identify triggers and eliminate them from the child's environment as much as possible. For example, a child who has experienced a natural disaster should not watch the event replayed on the news.

Provide a stable, predictable environment. For example, getting back into a school routine can be very helpful.

Provide an atmosphere that is neither intense nor emotionally intrusive. Don't ask too many probing questions. Be available to talk and answer questions about what happened. Give the child the words he needs to talk about his feelings and about what happened.

Provide soothing experiences. Be sure the child's day includes rocking, singing, talking, and fun, easy play. Make soothing activities part of regular activities, and be available when the child is upset or distressed. When soothing activities are part of the curriculum, children learn how to manage small amounts of anxiety before they spin out of control. Soothing activities may be especially anxiety-reducing around naptime. You may need to spend a little extra time helping a child who's experiencing trauma settle down.

Understand and recognize the symptoms of PTSD. When negative behaviors occur, help redirect the child in a positive way. Be patient with the child who seems to have regressed after a trauma. Instead of saying, "But, Maria, you know how to tie your shoes already," say, "I know it's hard, and everyone needs a little extra help sometimes. You'll be able to do it again when you're feeling better."

Separation Anxiety Disorder

Two-year-old Carlos comes from a very close-knit family. Because his new baby brother has significant developmental delays, his mother has had less time to spend with Carlos. She's been leaving him at his grandmother's house while she takes his brother to his many doctor and therapy appointments. Carlos is having more and more trouble saying good-bye to his mother in the morning. He screams, cries, and tries to hold on to her leg. He continues to cry for almost twenty minutes after she leaves and sometimes becomes so upset that he throws up. When a provider tries to hold him and soothe him, he resists, instead straining to look out the window to see if his mother might magically reappear. Although he eventually stops crying, he isn't very interested in the activities in the room. All day long he asks, "Mama? Mama?" He has trouble falling asleep at naptime and sometimes wakes up crying as if from a nightmare, asking for his mama.

TYPICAL SYMPTOMS

The DSM-IV-TR and DC:0–3R diagnostic criteria for separation anxiety disorder are similar. Older infants and toddlers often are somewhat anxious when separating from home or from primary caregivers. This type of separation anxiety is developmentally appropriate at this stage. Unusually high levels of anxiety in an older child, however, may be a sign of separation anxiety disorder.

Before a clinician diagnoses separation anxiety disorder, he or she will make sure that symptoms have been present persistently for at least four weeks and that the symptoms have caused significant distress or have gotten in the way of the child's ability to function at home or at school. To be diagnosed with this disorder, the child also needs to exhibit at least three of the following symptoms (adapted from the DSM-IV-TR and the DC:0–3R):

- The child often breaks down when he has to leave the house or when he's left with others. This may happen even before the separation, such as when the parent puts the child in the car seat in the morning. It may be impossible to soothe infants and toddlers. They may fight going to the provider when the parent leaves. If the child is very distressed, he might do something to hurt himself, such as banging his head on the floor or biting his arm. He might also try to hit or bite the provider.

- The child worries a lot that something might make her caregivers disappear from her life. She may worry that her caregivers will forget to pick her up from school or that they'll be kidnapped and she'll never see them again.

- The child may fight against going to school or being left anywhere by his caregiver. He may cry, hide, or struggle against getting ready to go.

- The child tries her best not to let the caregiver out of her sight. She may follow her caregiver around the house constantly in order to prevent separation. When outside the house, she may cling to her caregiver's leg or hand.

- The child can't fall asleep unless a caregiver is in the room.

- The child has frequent nightmares about being separated from his caregivers or has other scary dreams.

- A baby or young toddler might vomit or get a bad case of hiccups when the caregiver leaves. Older children might say they have a headache or stomachache or that they're going to throw up.

CAUSES

Separation anxiety disorder, which is more common in close-knit families, may be a reaction to a significant change or loss in the child's life, such as:

- Sudden loss (other than through death) of a caregiver or a pet. A child may also experience loss with a divorce, if a caregiver is hospitalized, if a caregiver goes to jail or rehab, or if the caregiver has to leave the child with others for a long period of time.

- Changing schools. Some children also react strongly when a favorite provider leaves or when she moves to a new classroom.

- Moving to a new house.

- Changes in the rituals and routines of daily life. Examples include the caregiver going back to work, a partner moving into the home, or the caregiver changing from day shift to night shift at work.

- The birth of a new sibling.

TREATMENT

For very young children, treatment is likely to include a combination of therapy for the child alone and therapy for the primary caregiver and child together. Sometimes family counseling as well as individual sessions for the child are used. Individual sessions can

- help the child gradually feel more independent and safe when the caregiver is away;

- help the child develop social and emotional skills—for example, recognizing and labeling emotions, expressing feelings through play, and learning ways to self-soothe.

In sessions for the caregiver and child together, the therapist can

- help the caregiver understand the disorder and make changes to routines or environment to help support the child;

- help the caregiver learn new ways to handle the child's emotions and behaviors;

- watch the interactions between the caregiver and the child, particularly noting what happens at separation times. The therapist and caregiver may work together to create a good-bye routine or other interventions for the home;

- observe how healthy the attachment is between the caregiver and the child. The therapist and caregiver can plan together how to strengthen the attachment relationship between the caregiver and the child.

Therapy is typically the first line of intervention. In rare cases, when the anxiety is very severe, a doctor may prescribe medication.

CLASSROOM AND CHILD CARE SETTING STRATEGIES

Stay in communication with caregivers. Children improve most when all of their adult caregivers work together as a united team. Children with separation anxiety disorders require consistency, and they need to know that all the adults in their life are in constant communication. For suggestions about establishing and maintaining communication with caregivers, see chapter 4.

Provide rituals and routines to help children feel safe and secure. Routines help children predict what will happen next and allow them to feel more control. Help the caregiver develop a regular good-bye routine for leaving his child in the morning. For example, first they hug, then the daddy says bye-bye, then the toddler waves bye-bye, and then the daddy smiles and says, "See you later" and leaves the room. Such routines often are as helpful for the caregiver as they are for the child. Posting a schedule that states when the child will be picked up from school and by whom can be helpful for some children.

Support the caregiver during the transition to school or child care. It can be very hard for a caregiver to leave a screaming child who's begging her to stay. Make yourself available by walking over and greeting the child and the caregiver. The child may not want to go to you at first. Get down to the child's level and welcome her. Tell her about the fun things you have for her to do that day. After a few minutes of comforting from the caregiver, encourage the caregiver to begin the good-bye routine you've worked on together. Hoping to avoid a scene, caregivers sometimes try to "sneak away" when the child isn't looking. Help the caregiver understand that leaving without saying good-bye often makes a child even more anxious next time. Make sure that the caregiver says good-bye and tells the child who will pick her up later that day.

Help the crying, screaming child complete the transition and settle in. The transition could follow these steps:

- Begin by letting the child hear that you know how he feels. Say something like "You miss your mommy. You want to go with her." Reflecting a child's feelings back to him often helps him begin to regain control.

- After a few moments of empathizing, try to direct the child to a favorite activity or an interesting new item. You might say something like "Let's go find some fun things to do until Nana comes to pick you up. Come, let's look in the water table." If this doesn't work, offer soothing activities such as rocking, singing, or reading together. Be sure to include soothing activities throughout the entire day, not just when the child is upset.

Designate a primary "go to" person for the child. If possible, choose the provider to whom the child seems naturally drawn. This person's role will be to help foster development of the provider-child bond, which is very important for children with separation anxiety disorder. This "go to" provider should be the one who

- spends dedicated time every day doing one-on-one activities with the child, such as reading a book together in the rocker, engaging the child in activities, singing a lullaby to the child at rest time, or pushing the child on a swing;

- soothes the child when she is upset or hurt;

- does as much of the physical caregiving for the child as possible, such as feeding, cleaning, diapering, changing clothes, putting to sleep;

- does most of the redirection and correction of the child's behaviors.

Help children learn how to identify, label, and manage their emotions. You can accomplish this when you:

- help the child understand that many children miss their families, and talk at group time about how children miss their families and how their families miss them;

- teach children strategies to manage being away from caregivers and invite them to write notes or draw pictures to take home;

- help children understand that caregivers exist even when they're out of sight. For example, have the class write and illustrate a big book about what caregivers do while children are at school.

Foster the connection between home and the care setting. Some examples of how to do this include:

- Ask the caregiver to leave with the child a family picture that he can carry around with him during the day. Post family pictures at a child's eye level on the walls of the room.

- Encourage caregivers to leave with the child something such as an old wallet, a scarf, or an extra set of keys. This "left item" will reassure the child that the caregiver will be back. Surprisingly, while children may worry that the caregiver will forget to come back for them, many trust that their caregiver will come back for a personal item.

Give children personal attention and extra support around naptime.

Generalized Anxiety Disorder

Four-year-old Aayalia has always been quiet and shy. She seems to worry all the time about little things. She needs frequent reassurance (much more often than any other child in the class) that she's doing things right. When she thinks she's doing something incorrectly, she gives up immediately, cries, or wrecks her project in frustration. Aayalia has trouble making friends. She cries every time another child says something that seems like a criticism or a rejection. She is very needy of the provider's time and attention.

TYPICAL SYMPTOMS

The DSM-IV-TR and DC:0–3R have similar diagnostic criteria for generalized anxiety disorder, in which a child worries about many different things, not just one event or one relationship. For a child to be diagnosed with generalized anxiety disorder, the anxiety has to be very distressful for the child and must get in the way of normal functioning in school or at home. Some medications, such as asthma medications or steroids, produce side effects similar to the symptoms of generalized anxiety disorder, so, as part of your effort to understand and address the child's anxious behavior, you may wish to ask what medications the child is taking. Symptoms for generalized anxiety disorder include (adapted from the DC:0–3R):

- The child is very worried or anxious most of the time. This anxiety has lasted for at least six months.

- The child finds it hard to cope with worries. He may keep going back to an adult for reassurances. For example, a child might constantly ask an adult whether his paintings, block structures, and sand castles are good.

- The child is anxious or worried during at least two different activities, in two different places, or with two different people.

- The child shows that he is anxious by one or more of the following behaviors:

  1. is fidgety or unable to sit still or lie still at rest time

  2. gets tired very easily

  3. is easily distracted

  4. is easily irritated and may have tantrums

  5. complains of physical aches and pains

  6. has trouble falling asleep or staying asleep at night, or tosses and turns in his sleep

CAUSES

According to some researchers, anxiety runs in families and is related to other disorders such as depression. There are also environmental causes. Persistent anxiety may be seen in children with difficulties in their primary attachment relationships or in children who face chronic environmental stressors, such as family instability, poverty, and violence in the neighborhood.

TREATMENT

The general treatment for generalized anxiety disorder is the same as for separation anxiety disorder. It includes individual therapy, family education, and joint family therapy. Medications may be considered if the anxiety is severe.

CLASSROOM AND CHILD CARE SETTING STRATEGIES

Stay in communication with caregivers. Children improve most when all of their adult caregivers work together as a united team. Children with generalized anxiety disorder require consistency, and they need to know that all the adults in their life are in constant communication. For suggestions about establishing and maintaining communication with caregivers, see chapter 4.

Provide rituals and routines to help children feel safe and secure.
Regular routines help reduce worries about what will happen next. Special
mini-routines throughout the day can help a child feel more confident that
what he is doing is right. For example, if, during family-style dining, the regular routine is that all bowls are passed and all children are served before eating begins, he won't worry every day about whether it's time to begin eating.

Support the caregiver during the transition to school or child care. It
can be very hard for a caregiver to leave a screaming child who's begging her
to stay. Make yourself available by walking over and greeting the child and the
caregiver. The child may not want to go to you at first. Get down to the child's
level and welcome her. Tell her about the fun things you have for her to do
that day. After a few minutes of comforting from the caregiver, encourage the
caregiver to begin the good-bye routine you've worked on together. Hoping
to avoid a scene, caregivers sometimes try to "sneak away" when the child isn't
looking. Help the caregiver understand that leaving without saying good-bye
often makes a child even more anxious next time. Make sure that the caregiver says good-bye and tells the child who will pick her up later that day.

Designate a primary "go to" person for the child. This may be the
provider to whom the child seems naturally drawn. This person should provide most of the interventions and attachment activities and be available as the
main comforter.

**Help all the children in the group recognize, label, and manage anxious
feelings.** Singling out the anxious child for "special instruction" may only
serve to increase his feeling that something is wrong. You can help all children
with strategies such as:

- Teaching relaxation techniques such as "Stop, take a deep breath,
  and relax," a technique developed by early childhood author and
  presenter Becky Bailey (Bailey 2001).

- Talking at group time about how everyone has worries and fears, and
  then modeling the process by saying something like "Yesterday, I
  heard some sudden loud thunder and it really scared me. Has anyone else ever felt scared?"

- Brainstorming with children about different things they can do to
  help themselves if they feel worried. You might start the conversation
  by saying, "When I got scared by the thunder, I found my cat and
  petted her. Then I felt better. How do you help yourself feel better?"

Don't be surprised if many of the children say the same thing that you did. Children learn from modeling. If nobody is coming up with original ideas, you might say, "Another time I was worried, I talked to my grandma about it. Then I felt better." When children have trouble suggesting strategies for soothing themselves, it's a sign that they don't know how to do it. Introduce new strategies with appropriate picture books, puppet play, and play-acting.

Help children learn problem-solving skills. You may want to illustrate interactions with a story or puppets and then have children role-play. You can choose a topic with the anxious child in mind. For example, focus on how to ask another child to play or what to do if something spills at snack.

Be patient with anxious children. They may need a great deal of reassurance and feedback that they are doing a good job. Try to offer positive feedback before they ask for it.

Help the child feel successful and capable.

- Don't overwhelm a child with an activity that is beyond her abilities. Challenge her just a little and support her as she takes each step. For example, if she's been successful at six-piece puzzles, invite her to try a twelve-piece puzzle with you.

- Keep a journal with the child to record her accomplishments at the end of the day. Add photos of her learning new things and doing things well. Pictures are often more powerful than words. For example, help her remember that she put the doll's shirt on all by herself. Show her the digital picture you took and ask her to dictate a caption for it. From time to time, read the journal with her or send it home for her to share with her family.

CHAPTER 8: Mood Disorders

Everyone has ups and downs. We see this perhaps most dramatically in young children when they go through the so-called terrible twos. But children who are depressed, grieving, or suffering from pediatric bipolar disorder have changes in mood and behavior that are unexpected and persist over time.

Depression

Over the past few months, four-year-old Aio has become more withdrawn and tearful. She gets upset over little things and cries, saying, "Nobody likes me" or "I'm just stupid." She used to love to paint and draw, but now it's much harder to get her motivated to start projects. Aio seems tired all the time, but she can't lie still and has trouble falling asleep at naptime. When really tired, her mood can become irritable and whiny. Her appetite has decreased and she's not eating much. The other kids have stopped asking her to play, because she either says no or plays with little enthusiasm.

TYPICAL SYMPTOMS

Depression can range from mild to severe. According to the DSM-IV-TR, children must have at least five of the following symptoms to be diagnosed as having severe or major depression (adapted from the DSM-IV-TR):

- Are sad or irritable for most of the day, day after day, for at least two weeks. An older child might say, "I'm sad." Young children are more likely to show signs of sadness such as weeping or a sad facial expression.

- Don't want to do the things they are usually excited about, and even when they do get involved, they don't seem to be having fun.

- Have major changes in their eating habits—they may gain or lose a lot of weight (usually 5 percent of body weight in one month)

- Develop sleep problems not typical for a child or for a child this age, such as having trouble falling asleep or staying asleep, or sleeping too much.

- Are restless and agitated—or, the opposite: move or talk more slowly than usual.

- Feel tired all the time or feel worthless or guilty for no reason. An older child might make comments such as "I'm so dumb." Children might also act out these feelings in their play.

- Have trouble making simple decisions, like what color paper to use. They are often less able to solve simple problems such as undoing a knot in their shoe. They may have trouble staying with a task, such as finishing a puzzle.

- Talk a lot about death or dying or try to hurt themselves.

Young children with depression may also be more irritable, complain more about stomachaches or headaches, or have more aggressive behaviors than adults who have depression.

CAUSES

Depression in young children is probably caused by a combination of genetics and environment. For children who are biologically vulnerable to depression, the following events may trigger an episode:

- moving
- birth of a sibling
- fighting between adults in the home
- divorce in the family

Mood Disorder Symptoms at a Glance

Depression	Prolonged bereavement	Bipolar disorder
• frequent sad or irritable moods • cries a lot • unmotivated and lacks joy • low self-esteem • tired all the time • difficulty sleeping • change in appetite • frequent stomach-aches or headaches • aggressive behavior	• recently experienced a significant loss, such as the death of a parent • depressive symptoms last more than two months after the loss • frequently talks about the lost loved one	• frequent and intense mood swings • increased irritability later in the day • difficulty sleeping • easily frustrated • throws tantrums • aggressive • shows oppositional behavior • experiences nightmares or night terrors • exhibits separation anxiety

Other difficulties that might look like a mood disorder include:

- problems in the primary attachment relationship

- anxiety disorders

- posttraumatic stress disorder (PTSD)

- oppositional defiant disorder

- regulatory disorder

- attention-deficit/hyperactivity disorder (ADHD)

- loss of a loved one through death or leaving the household

- mental illness in another member of the child's household

- other stressors

TREATMENT

Depression in young children is usually treated with professional counseling. Any counseling should include the child's family, because young children's lives are closely interwoven with their primary caregivers. For therapy to be effective, caregivers need to know what to do at home to help their child. When depression is severe or doesn't improve with counseling, a psychiatrist may prescribe an antidepressant medication for the child.

CLASSROOM AND CHILD CARE SETTING STRATEGIES

Stay in communication with caregivers. Children improve most when all of their adult caregivers work together as a united team. Children with depression require consistency, and they need to know that all the adults in their life are communicating and working together. For suggestions about establishing and maintaining communication with caregivers, see chapter 4.

Spend special time with the child to build a strong and safe relationship. Children with depression need an adult they can depend on who accepts them unconditionally. Ways to build these bonds include lap reading, having the child be your special helper in setting up snack, and personally greeting the child every morning and saying a warm good-bye to him at the end of the day.

Help children learn and talk about feelings and personal experiences. Listen to, reflect, and label feelings. Plan activities to help children express their feelings. Have children draw pictures of emotions and identify emotions of characters in picture books. Notice other children's emotions in the room ("I see Lucy is hiding under the table. I think she might have gotten scared when that fire truck went by. Let's go see.").

Create an environment that is safe and inviting for sharing thoughts. Validate children's feelings when they express them. By doing so, you send them the message that their emotions are important. For example, when Damien says he's scared of dogs, you might say, "Yes, some people are afraid of dogs they don't know" instead of saying "There's nothing to be scared of."

Encourage the child to get involved in activities. Have some of the child's favorite activities available every day. The more active and involved the child is, the better she will feel. Smile or chat briefly with the child when she gets involved in an activity. Your positive attention makes it more likely that the child will repeat the behavior.

Plan some one-on-one time with the child every day. Gradually begin to include other children in the play.

Prolonged Bereavement

Jorge is three years old. His father died unexpectedly over the summer. Now Jorge, his mother, and his siblings are living with extended family. Jorge, who rarely smiles or shows much emotion, is quiet and withdrawn much of the time. He's tired all the time and sleeps a lot. Sometimes he'll surprise the teacher by coming over and talking about his dad. He says things like "My daddy is in heaven now. Can I call him on the phone?" or, after seeing a picture of a truck, "My daddy used to drive me in his truck." Jorge rarely gets involved in classroom activities, and the other kids tend to ignore him. Occasionally he'll hit or yell at a child who upsets him. Once, he threw sand at a boy who tried to play with him on the playground.

TYPICAL SYMPTOMS

The symptoms of depression and prolonged bereavement are the same. Prolonged bereavement is the diagnosis given when a child has lost a significant loved one and is grieving (that is, showing the symptoms of depression listed previously) for longer than the time considered "normal" within her culture. Generally, psychologists consider two months or more as a long time.

In very young children, the process of grieving can be complicated by the fact that young children are incapable of understanding the permanence of death. Sometimes they'll talk about going off to be with the dead loved one, or they'll talk of wanting to die to be with that person. For older people, thoughts like these would be signs of serious problems. In children, such thinking is often related to their lack of understanding and should be addressed using sensitive and culturally appropriate information.

CAUSES

No one knows why some children struggle longer than others and show severe signs of grief and depression after the loss of a significant loved one. Factors that might affect the intensity and length of a child's grief include

- whether the loss was sudden and unexpected or whether the child had time to say good-bye;

- how the surviving caregivers and family are handling their own grief;

- how caregivers acknowledge and handle the loss with the child;

- whether significant changes occurred after the loss, such as having to move or to change schools or being affected by financial problems in the family.

TREATMENT

The treatment approaches for depression and prolonged bereavement are similar. Individual and family therapy is usually recommended. Treatment should specifically address the loss and grieving process. Although medication may be used if the depression becomes very severe or is significantly getting in the way of the child's development, medication without therapy and support may have limited effectiveness over the long term.

CLASSROOM AND CHILD CARE SETTING STRATEGIES

Stay in communication with caregivers. Children improve most when all of their adult caregivers work together as a united team. Children with prolonged bereavement require consistency, and they need to know that all the adults in their life are in regular communication. For suggestions about establishing and maintaining communication with primary caregivers, see chapter 4. Also, plan to meet with the family to discuss ways to talk to the child about death, being sure that what you suggest is appropriate for their cultural and religious beliefs.

Help the child understand that she is not responsible for the death. Because children are so egocentric, they often believe that something they did caused the person to die. Reassure the child as often as needed that her father didn't die because of anything she or her father did (for example, have angry feelings toward her).

Refer to the classroom and child care setting strategies pertaining to depression. There you'll find ideas about how to increase engagement, how to encourage expression of feelings, and other possible interventions.

Bipolar Disorder

Four-year-old Rudy's behavior is often unpredictable and difficult to manage. Sometimes, during the same day, he'll be withdrawn and tearful, clinging to the provider for reassurance, and later he'll get into fights, talk back to the teacher, throw a tantrum, and refuse to follow directions. His irritability and activity level seem to get worse over the course of the day. Rudy often has difficulty paying attention and is easily frustrated when things are a little difficult. Once he's upset, it's hard for him to calm down, even with help. He talks all the time and often seems revved up and unable to sit still. He has difficulty settling down for naptime and has frequent nightmares. Rudy is a bright child who can be very charming and creative, but his provider is feeling unsure about how to help him in the classroom.

TYPICAL SYMPTOMS

Bipolar disorder is a controversial diagnosis in very young children. One complication is that the DSM-IV-TR has not set different criteria for pediatric bipolar disorder and adult bipolar disorder. Therefore, to be diagnosed with this disorder, a child is assessed based on the symptoms of adult bipolar disorder. To meet DSM-IV-TR criteria for a manic episode, the person must have at least one manic or hypomanic (less-severe manic) episode lasting for at least one week (or a shorter time if the person is hospitalized). Manic symptoms for an adult include (adapted from the DSM-IV-TR):

- Exhibiting extreme excitement or irritability. The extremely excited person usually describes having an intense feeling of euphoria, as though nothing can ever go wrong and the world is a wonderful, amazing place.

- Showing high energy and increased activity levels. The person often is extremely active for many hours at a time, accomplishing a number of things, such as cleaning the house, jogging several miles, and then starting an art project.

- Needing less sleep. The person may claim to need only three or four hours of sleep each night to feel rested and ready to start the next day.

- Constantly talking about many ideas. The person's speech often comes across as "pressured," so much so that others have a hard time getting a word in edgewise.

- Being easily distracted. The person keeps getting distracted by little things that others don't normally notice, such as a rug or a small movement. A person having a manic episode has a hard time concentrating for very long.

- Doing things for fun even if they're dangerous. Possibilities can include using drugs, engaging in sexual activity, going on spending sprees, and driving recklessly.

Most people with this disorder also have periods of major depression (see the previous section on depression for a list of symptoms). Some people have symptoms of mania and major depression at the same time; this combination is called a *mixed episode*.

Recent research suggests that early onset, or pediatric, bipolar disorder exists and is different from adult bipolar disorder. It may be a subtype of bipolar disorder with different characteristics and outcomes than later-onset bipolar disorder (Mick et al. 2003; Papolos and Papolos 2002). Characteristics of a child with pediatric bipolar disorder include the following (Papolos and Papolos 2002):

- Has changes in mood from mania/irritability to depression that may occur rapidly and many times a day. The child may be mostly irritable, with few periods of relief in between.

- Often has low energy in the morning, with increased activity level and irritability during the day and into the evening

- Has difficulty with sleeping, nightmares, night terrors, and bedwetting (enuresis)

- Experiences intense fear when separating from a caregiver

- Is easily frustrated and has a great deal of difficulty managing strong emotions

- Exhibits aggressive and oppositional behaviors, including physical aggression toward others, tantrums, and refusal to follow rules or requests. (Be careful not to confuse the acting out and oppositional behaviors that often show up at around age two with symptoms of bipolar disorder.)

- Often comes from a family with a history of bipolar disorder, other mood disorders, and/or alcoholism

Diagnosing pediatric bipolar disorder requires the skills of an experienced clinician. And making the right diagnosis is especially important, because the medications that are helpful for treating ADHD and depression can be harmful to a child with bipolar disorder. Receiving the wrong medication can even lead to the child being hospitalized.

CAUSES

Children with bipolar disorder on both sides of the family and with a family history of alcoholism have a higher likelihood of being diagnosed with pediatric bipolar disorder (Papolos and Papolos 2002). A child's environment also can trigger symptoms or can make symptoms worse. Trauma, a poor relationship between the child and the primary caregiver, harsh parenting, poverty, or family stress can worsen symptoms and can make the disorder harder to manage.

TREATMENT

Obtaining proper assessment and diagnosis is always the first step in addressing mental health concerns, but finding mental health specialists with training and experience in pediatric bipolar disorder can be difficult.

Children with bipolar disorder need a lot of support and a team approach. An experienced child psychiatrist is needed to prescribe medication. Children with bipolar disorder are often helped with mood stabilizers such as lithium or Depakote and some antipsychotic drugs such as Risperdal.

Many children with bipolar disorder also can be helped by individual and family therapy. Individual therapy can help them manage their emotions and develop better coping skills. Educating and involving primary *and* secondary caregivers is essential. Caregivers need information about pediatric bipolar disorder. They also need help with accepting the illness and with implementing appropriate interventions and behavior plans at home and in child care and school settings, especially if the child is in these settings most of the day.

CLASSROOM AND CHILD CARE SETTING STRATEGIES

Stay in communication with caregivers. Children improve most when all of their adult caregivers work together as a united team. Children with bipolar disorder require consistency, and they need to know that all the adults in their life are in regular communication. For suggestions about establishing and maintaining communication with caregivers, see chapter 4.

Provide routine and predictability. Children with bipolar disorder may struggle with change and transition. Always prepare them in advance, especially for a big change such as a field trip. Talk about what is going to happen and show them pictures, if possible. Remind them as the day approaches. Make transitions during the day easier by using a routine warning, such as sounding a chime or playing special music to signal transition time. A warning gives the child time to prepare for the change.

Help the child develop a strong attachment with one particular provider. Though attachment is important for all children, children with bipolar disorder need extra support and help with their emotions. The stronger the attachment you develop with a child, the easier time you'll have setting limits.

Create an environment that helps children be aware of, and label, emotions.

Help children feel that it is safe and appropriate to talk about feelings and experiences.

Identify triggers. Be a good observer. Pay attention to what happens to trigger a tantrum or a meltdown. This will help you prevent repeat incidents.

Be on the lookout for meltdowns. If you see a meltdown coming, remove the child from the situation and help her to problem-solve, or give her alternatives. For example, say, "I saw that you really wanted to go down the slide next. Jamal's taking his turn now. I'll hold your hand until it's your turn." Or "I can see you're getting upset. Let's see what else we can do. I know; here's your favorite thing." Or "I can see you really want to use that toy. Let's ask Alicia if she's done with it."

Try to keep a meltdown from escalating once it's started. Label the child's feelings and acknowledge his pain. Provide and model soothing behaviors. Remember that different soothing behaviors work for different children.

Try having the child rock in a chair, sit with a special toy or blanket, sit in your lap for a short period, or look at a picture of a family member.

Take a child who is having a meltdown to a quiet, calm area with no distractions. Sit nearby, label her feelings, and let her know that you're there to help when she's ready. Avoid leaving the child by herself during a meltdown, or the meltdown may get worse.

Remain patient and supportive, and be consistent as you enforce limits. Some children with bipolar disorder will challenge limits. Remember that they're not trying to make your life difficult; they're in a great deal of pain and have few, if any, ways of dealing with the intensity of their experiences.

Acknowledge positive behaviors. Children with bipolar disorder tend to get attention when they're having behavioral difficulties. So they don't think that only misbehavior gets noticed, give them lots of attention for positive behaviors.

Encourage children who are in a depressed mood to join in fun activities. Refer to the section on depression for more ideas about how to work with a child who's in a depressed phase.

CHAPTER 9: Attention-Deficit and Disruptive-Behavior Disorders

From time to time, all children are oppositional, act aggressively, and have difficulty paying attention. These behaviors occur most often when children are tired, hungry, stressed, or upset. They may argue, disobey, hit, push, walk away, or not listen. Saying no, hitting others on occasion, and having a short attention span are considered normal behaviors for young children. However, the behavior of some children goes well beyond typical uncooperative behaviors and may be symptomatic of a disorder.

Because attention-deficit/hyperactivity disorder, or ADHD, is a household word nowadays, many providers, caregivers, and clinicians are quick to make this diagnosis when a child seems to have difficulty paying attention or sitting still. But a child can have attention difficulties for a number of reasons. To rule out the presence of problems other than ADHD, a careful examination must be done.

Attention-Deficit/Hyperactivity Disorder

Four-year-old Bobi runs around constantly. He cannot sit still for more than a few seconds and constantly gets up, walks around, and touches things during circle time. He even has trouble sitting in his seat for lunch. Bobi will start an activity and then quickly move to another before ever really getting started on the first. The other children get annoyed with him because he interrupts, butts in, and messes up their projects. It often takes physical touch to get his attention, and he needs constant reminders to complete a task. He seems scattered almost all the time. He drops and forgets his toys and other belongings frequently. Bobi talks all the time, but he doesn't stick with a particular topic. He gets very upset and frustrated when he has to wait his turn and often has a tantrum if he's made to wait. Although his teachers generally think he's a good boy and like him, Bobi requires so much supervision and attention that they become frustrated and exhausted.

TYPICAL SYMPTOMS

Although we usually think of ADHD as one disorder, the DSM-IV-TR recognizes several variations of ADHD. In the first variation, the child has attention difficulties. In the second, the child is hyperactive and impulsive. A child with the third variation—a combination of the other two—has both a very short attention span and hyperactive/impulsive behavior.

The DSM-IV-TR has several general guidelines for diagnosing ADHD:

- The behaviors must be disruptive.

- The behaviors must be developmentally and culturally inappropriate.

- The behaviors must be present for at least six months.

- The behaviors must happen in more than one setting—for example, both at home *and* at school. If the behavior occurs only at home or only at school, the child does not meet the criteria for ADHD.

- The behaviors must start before the child is seven years old.

To be diagnosed with the inattentive form of ADHD, the child must have at least six of the following symptoms (adapted from the DSM-IV-TR):

- does not pay close attention to details

- has trouble keeping attention on tasks—for example, moves from the paint table to the sand tray to the dramatic play area without ever completing a task or play theme

Attention-Deficit and Disruptive-Behavior Symptoms at a Glance

Attention-deficit/ hyperactivity disorder (ADHD)	Oppositional defiant disorder (ODD)	Conduct disorder
• poor attention to activities • does not seem to listen • easily distracted • "on the go" all the time • can't sit still • talks all the time • impulsive • can't wait for a turn	• argues with adults • refuses to follow rules • gets angry all the time • easily irritated • displays mean, hurtful behavior • deliberately annoys people	• physically aggressive or cruel to people or animals • destroys others' things or sets fires • lies and steals • runs away from home • stays out all night • little or no remorse or empathy for others

Other difficulties or characteristics that resemble attention-deficit or disruptive-behavior disorders include the following:

- problems in the primary attachment relationship

- aggression and poor attention secondary to other delays, such as language development or other learning disorders

- posttraumatic stress disorder (PTSD)

- other anxiety disorders

- depression

- aggression and poor attention (secondary to lack of appropriate stimulation for the intellectually gifted)

- does not seem to listen when spoken to directly

- often fails to follow instructions or finish work or chores

- often has trouble figuring out the steps to complete an activity—for example, stares at and fiddles with items on the table until the provider sits next to her and tells her to first put the glue on the paper, then pick a feather, and then put the feather on the glue spot

- avoids or dislikes tasks that take a lot of concentration for a long time—for example, never wants to try puzzles or build a house with blocks, preferring instead to run, jump, get into something quickly, and then move on

- often loses things needed for tasks

- is often easily distracted—for example, has trouble focusing on a task because he gets distracted when someone moves, or a bright object catches his eye, or he hears bits of background noise

- is forgetful

Again according to the DSM-IV-TR, to be diagnosed as the hyperactive-impulsive type, the child must have at least six of the following symptoms:

- exhibits hyperactivity

- often fidgets or squirms

- gets up when she's supposed to be sitting

- runs and climbs when not appropriate

- has trouble playing quietly

- is constantly "on the go" or "driven by a motor"

- talks excessively

- is impulsive

- blurts out answers before questions have been completed

- has trouble waiting for a turn

- interrupts others' conversations or games

To be diagnosed with the combined type of ADHD (inattention *and* hyperactive/impulsive), the DSM-IV-TR specifies that the child must exhibit at least six symptoms from each list.

CAUSES

ADHD probably is caused by a combination of genetics and environment. Research suggests that children with ADHD have impaired functioning in the part of the brain that controls reasoning, organizing, planning, and paying attention (Weyandt 2005). Research also shows that ADHD may be hereditary; that is, children with ADHD are more likely to have parents who have ADHD.

Environment also plays a role in ADHD. Research on attachment and trauma in early childhood suggests that environment can influence brain development. Trauma or attachment problems leave children vulnerable to developing difficulties with self-regulation, including attention span (Schore 2001).

Many children diagnosed with ADHD have a combination of challenges. They may, at the same time, also have other diagnoses, such as learning disabilities, depression, or oppositional defiant disorder.

TREATMENT

Medication is usually the first line of treatment for children with ADHD, since it has been shown to reduce symptoms. Some commonly prescribed medications are Ritalin, Adderall, and Strattera.

Research shows that behavioral interventions at school and at home also help the child. Children with ADHD need support to learn how to concentrate, how to break tasks down into manageable parts, and how to organize their world. Primary caregivers and providers who understand ADHD and who learn behavioral strategies play critical roles in the success of the overall treatment plan.

The family environment is particularly important for young children with ADHD. Preschoolers with ADHD have poorer outcomes when they have multiple caregivers, caregivers who have a poor understanding of development, or caregivers who don't help them learn how to self-soothe or self-regulate (Fraser 2002).

CLASSROOM AND CHILD CARE SETTING STRATEGIES

The following suggestions are specific to working with children who have been diagnosed with ADHD. For more suggestions, refer to the classroom and child care setting strategies for ADHD, Oppositional Defiant Disorder (ODD), and conduct disorder listed at the end of this chapter.

Give children with ADHD something to fiddle with during times you expect them to sit still. For example, let the child hold and squeeze a ball during circle time. This can often be enough to help the child focus. If he needs more support, try having him sit next to an adult.

Give children support to complete complex tasks. Break down tasks into as many small steps as possible. Monitor a child's progress, and remind her of the next step in the process. Give her a lot of practice in successfully completing multistep tasks. Repeated successful practice helps children learn how to break large tasks into smaller bits and lets them experience the positive feelings that come with accomplishment.

Oppositional Defiant Disorder (ODD)

From the beginning, Ramon's teachers struggled to help him become comfortable with the routines and expectations of the classroom. He resisted all their efforts. They were frustrated and irritated with this three-year-old boy who seemed to defy their every request and suggestion. When asked to do something or when a limit was set, Ramon openly defied them, said no, called them stupid, and ran off. He got angry very easily and went out of his way to annoy others or to seek revenge. When providers set limits, Ramon would have a loud tantrum. If providers forced the issue, he would kick and hit them.

TYPICAL SYMPTOMS

For a child to be diagnosed with ODD, the DSM-IV-TR requires evidence of an ongoing pattern of uncooperative, defiant, and hostile behavior toward authority. This behavior has to seriously interfere with the child's day-to-day functioning and must persist over at least six months in order to fit the criteria. Typical symptoms include (adapted from the DSM-IV-TR):

- often loses temper

- argues with adults

- actively defies or refuses to comply with adults' requests or rules

- deliberately annoys people

- blames others for his or her own mistakes or misbehavior

- is touchy or easily annoyed by others

- is angry, resentful, spiteful, and vindictive

CAUSES

Some researchers believe that children diagnosed with ODD and conduct disorder (a related disorder described in the next section) are hard-wired differently than other children. These children may have brain differences that leave them more negative, more aggressive, and less adaptable (Thomas and Chess 1977; Bates et al. 1991). There may be a genetic link. The DSM-IV-TR notes that children diagnosed with ODD and conduct disorder tend to have a close adult family member who's been diagnosed with ODD, conduct disorder, antisocial personality disorder, ADHD, or depression or who has a history of substance abuse.

Factors other than genetics may play a larger role. For example, research has shown a possible link between ODD and exposure to chronic stress associated with poverty, neighborhood violence, family problems, unemployment, and crowded living situations. Also, parents of children with ODD and conduct disorder tend to have higher levels of depression and, in turn, lack confidence in their caregiving skills and exhibit inconsistency with regard to discipline. Research suggests that early attachment and caregiver education play a large role in a child's behaviors. Caregivers of children with ODD tend to discipline with hitting, yelling, and threats (Linfoot, Martin, and Stephenson 1999; Webster-Stratton 1993). Evidence also shows that children with ODD lack social skills (Webster-Stratton 1993). What's not clear is whether this skill deficit is a cause of symptoms or the result of poor attachment and interrupted social-emotional growth. Each of these many factors seems to make a contribution to the development of diagnosable problems and to the long-term outcome for these children.

TREATMENT

Treatment of a child with ODD should be comprehensive and include individual treatment for parents and caregivers; caregiver education about the disorder; caregiver behavior management skills training; behavioral plans and interventions for the child in school; and individual treatment for the child. Also, medication to treat aggressive symptoms can be considered if the behavior concerns are severe.

CLASSROOM AND CHILD CARE SETTING STRATEGIES

See the classroom and child care setting strategies for ADHD, ODD, and conduct disorder at the end of this chapter.

Conduct Disorder

Five-year-old Starr seems to enjoy hurting others. She bullies the other kids on the playground and has caused several bloody noses. The other children are afraid of Starr and try to stay away from her. One day the teacher found Starr under the jungle gym trying to pressure another child into pulling down her pants. Another time, the class gerbil was found in its cage with its tail cut off. The teachers don't know who did it, but they strongly suspect it was Starr. She deliberately destroys other children's toys and projects and doesn't seem to care or feel sorry when she makes other children cry. She never admits to doing anything wrong, even when it's obvious that she's done it. Nothing the teachers do seems to improve her behavior. The teachers don't know what to think of Starr. They are concerned and even a little fearful.

TYPICAL SYMPTOMS

Conduct disorder is characterized by a child who continually hurts people or animals, purposely destroys property, lies, and breaks vital rules. Adults usually describe children with conduct disorder as "delinquents" who lack concern or empathy for their victims. Conduct disorder is more common in boys than in girls. Although some symptoms may be present as early as age four or five, the disorder is not usually diagnosable until a child is in early adolescence. Younger children lack the physical strength, cognitive development, and sexual maturity to have all of the symptoms. In some cases, older children diagnosed with conduct disorder were diagnosed with oppositional defiant disorder when they were younger (DSM-IV-TR). However, children diagnosed with oppositional defiant disorder do not necessarily develop conduct disorder.

Typical symptoms of conduct disorder include (adapted from the DSM-IV-TR):

- serious aggression toward people and animals, including bullying, threatening, starting physical fights, using a weapon, physical cruelty, assault, or forceful sexual activity

- deliberate destruction of property, including breaking and destroying things and setting fires

- deceit, lying, or stealing, including breaking and entering and shoplifting, but not including occasionally fibbing or taking another child's toy

- serious rule violations, including running away from home, staying out all night, and frequently missing school, but not including minor "naughty" behaviors such as refusing to clean up a room or slamming a door when angry

Rarely would any of these symptoms apply to young children, who are still developing an understanding of truth and lying, private property, and stealing. Likewise, young children would have difficulty running away from home, being truant from school, or obtaining weapons. Because of these limitations, conduct disorder is rarely diagnosed in very young children.

CAUSES

As with ODD, some researchers believe that children diagnosed with conduct disorder are hard-wired differently than other children. These children may have brain differences that leave them more negative, more aggressive, and less adaptable (Thomas and Chess 1977; Bates et al. 1991). There may be a genetic link. The DSM-IV-TR also notes that children diagnosed with ODD and conduct disorder tend to have a close adult family member who's been diagnosed with ODD, conduct disorder, antisocial personality disorder, ADHD, or depression or who has a history of substance abuse.

Factors other than genetics may play a larger role; for example, exposure to chronic stress associated with poverty, neighborhood violence, family problems, unemployment, and crowded living situations. Also, parents of children with ODD and conduct disorder tend to have higher levels of depression and, in turn, lack confidence in their caregiving skills and exhibit inconsistency with regard to discipline. Each of these many factors seems to make a contribution to the development of diagnosable problems and to the long-term outcome for these children.

TREATMENT

Treatment of a child with conduct disorder should involve a comprehensive approach that provides individual treatment for parents and caregivers; caregiver education about the disorder; caregiver behavior management skills training; behavioral plans and interventions for the child in school; and individual treatment for the child. Also, medication to treat aggressive symptoms can be considered if the behavior concerns are severe.

CLASSROOM AND CHILD CARE SETTING STRATEGIES FOR ADHD, ODD, AND CONDUCT DISORDER

Stay in communication with caregivers. Children improve most when all of their adult caregivers work together as a united team. Children with ADHD, ODD, or conduct disorder require consistency, and they need to know that all the adults in their life are in constant communication. For suggestions about establishing and maintaining communication with caregivers, see chapter 4.

Support the development of attachment. The role of attachment with caregivers and providers is the basis on which all other interventions rest. Children with ODD, conduct disorder, or ADHD desperately need consistent, positive relationships with adults. Find opportunities to connect one-on-one with the child on a daily basis. Rub his back and sing a lullaby at rest time. Ask him to help you with a special task like moving a table. Look for a time when he's playing appropriately and ask him if you can join in for a few moments. Use active listening to let the child know you're really listening and caring. For an explanation of active listening, see pages 36–37.

Label and reflect on the child's emotions. Understanding emotions is the first step toward developing healthy, positive ways to manage them. For example, when Luo is throwing toys, say, "Luo, I can see that you are angry, but we need to stay safe here. Let me see if I can help you. Can you use your words to tell me that you are angry?"

Create a user-friendly environment. Impulsive, explosive, angry, inflexible, and inattentive children need structure, guidance, and support. Establish clear and consistent rules. Review the rules frequently and in simple terms. Use pictures and photos on the wall as reminders of what to do. For example, near the snack table, post a photo of a child wiping up a spill.

Role-play with children how to handle potentially difficult situations. For example, at group time play a transition game such as "Excuse me." Have the children sit in a tight circle. Call on one child to first come to the center of the circle and then go to one of the other children and say, "Excuse me." Guide the seated child in moving over to make space for the standing child to walk through and leave the circle. Frequent practice of social skills helps all the children in a classroom or child care setting speak the same "social language."

Reduce stress. Limit decorations on the walls. Keep toys neatly stored in bins. Don't play constant background music. Establish a calm place in the room—an area with very little stimulation or distraction where children can go when they're feeling overwhelmed. Soft pillows and a few cuddly toys in a corner screened off with netting would be enough to set an area apart as a quiet area. Invite children to use this area when they're getting agitated.

Give children who have difficulty transitioning an additional warning before starting the process. When there will be a change in routine, warn children in advance. Talk about what will happen and how it will be different from the activity they're leaving.

Support children's individual needs for learning. Provide support to help children successfully complete novel tasks or skills that are slightly beyond their current level. Be careful to avoid demands that are so beyond their skill level that their frustration will overwhelm them.

Pick your battles. Especially with extremely hostile and oppositional children, decide which rules are necessary for the good of the child and the classroom or setting, and avoid going to the mat over every little thing. Once you tell a child to do something, follow through in helping her complete it. If you ask a child to put her plate away and then fail to follow through when she doesn't do it, you give her permission to ignore your next request.

Recognize positive behavior. One of the most effective ways to eliminate negative behavior is to consciously acknowledge positive behavior—even attempts or partial completions of important goals. Consider keeping a journal of the child's accomplishments each day, and review it with him at the end of the day. Then send the journal of his successes home to his parents at the end of the week. When giving directions, help the child understand what it is that you want and how he can accomplish that. For example, instead of just saying "Don't leave your dirty plate on the table," say, "Pick up your plate and your cup and put them in the bucket. Then you can go play."

Teach basic social skills. Children with ODD or conduct disorder often struggle with how to interact with others successfully. Teach them how to understand nonverbal communication, how to enter and exit play, and how to take turns and listen to others. At large or small group time, you can model skills with puppets and have the children act out simple interactions with others. Take the opportunity to coach the child during center-based time and outdoor time. Stand nearby when the child tries to enter play with others. Talk aloud about what is happening. You might say, "Anthony wants the block now. He wants to know if you will give him the block. There you go; you gave him a turn. Oh, you want to show Anthony what you've made. Anthony, look what Ramon made." When you talk out loud about what is happening, you're facilitating and modeling how to make things happen. Over time, you may be able to encourage a child like Ramon to take more responsibility in this process.

Incorporate activities that promote self-regulation in a fun way. Introduce games such as "freeze" and "red light, green light." Include activities that require transition from gross to fine motor skills. For example, set up an obstacle course so the children have to run fast, put a peg in a hole, run fast again, and then put a block on a string. Play games that involve changing tempo—roll the ball fast, roll the ball slowly. Practice singing songs that include singing loudly and then singing softly.

Use guidelines for handling tantrums or aggression. For more detailed suggestions, refer to the classroom and child care setting strategies for helping children with bipolar disorder.

- Identify triggers.

- Identify ways to help the child calm down before the behavior escalates.

- Help the child work through a severe meltdown.

- Address the situation with the child after he's regained his composure.

Never physically restrain a child unless you're extremely concerned about harm to yourself, to the child acting out, or to another child. Preschool children are small. Even very aggressive behaviors, such as throwing chairs and toys, can be handled without physical restraint. Simply direct the child to a safe area and block his exit with your body.

CHAPTER 10: Pervasive Developmental Disorders

The most common diagnoses in this category are autism, Asperger's disorder (also known as Asperger's syndrome), and pervasive developmental disorder not otherwise specified (PDD-NOS). A diagnosis of PDD-NOS is given when a child has serious delays in social skills and communication but does not meet the full criteria for either autism or Asperger's disorder. The information about PDD-NOS is similar to that for autism and Asperger's, so it is not discussed separately. Rett's disorder and childhood disintegrative disorder are rare and are not discussed here.

Autism

Twenty-four-month-old Jermaine does not have any words yet but will sometimes point or grunt when he wants something. He stays in one area of the classroom all the time and plays with the same toys over and over. Although he passed his hearing tests, he doesn't respond if someone calls his name. The provider usually has to go over and touch him to get his attention. When other children try to play with him or touch his toys, he cries and has tantrums. He doesn't often make eye contact and isn't interested in the teacher or the other kids. Jermaine gets overstimulated and upset by ordinary things such as the woodchips on the playground or somebody brushing against him. Sometimes he falls hard and then gets up as if nothing happened. He has trouble following the routine of the classroom, especially if there are changes. Most often Jermaine seems to want to live in his own world.

Pervasive Developmental Disorder Symptoms at a Glance		
Autism	**Asperger's disorder**	**Pervasive developmental disorder not otherwise specified (PDD-NOS)**
• lack of interest in others • notably delayed language skills, including nonverbal skills • plays with toys the same way over and over • gets upset if routines are changed • strange body movements, such as hand flapping • delays in cognitive development and personal care skills • sensory sensitivities	• poor social skills but seems interested in others • talks a lot • has language basics but struggles with nonverbal communication and social language • very specific, repetitive interests • prefers routines	• serious delays in social and communication skills • does not meet full criteria for either autism or Asperger's disorder

Other difficulties that might look like pervasive developmental disorders include the following:

• problems in the primary attachment relationship
• regulatory disorders
• obsessive-compulsive disorder
• delays in social and cognitive development resulting from specific severe language delays
• hearing problems
• eccentricities associated with intellectual giftedness (most likely to occur with Asperger's disorder)

TYPICAL SYMPTOMS

The DSM-IV-TR diagnostic criteria focus on three main areas of concern: social interactions, communication delays, and repetitive behaviors. A child must have symptoms from all three of these areas to be diagnosed with autism, and some of the symptoms must be present before the child turns three years old. These symptoms include (adapted from the DSM-IV-TR):

Social interactions. Children with autism struggle with relationships. They tend to prefer to play by themselves a lot. They rarely share their experiences or successes with peers or adults and rarely respond to invitations to play or talk. As a result, they usually don't make friends. Children with autism may not be interested in family members, including their brothers and sisters. Families with autistic children will often say that their child doesn't like to be hugged, cuddled, or kissed as other children do, although the child may go to her primary caregiver for something to eat or because she's hurt. Some children with autism do like roughhousing or other gross motor activities that stimulate their sensory needs and will seek out others for these experiences.

Communication delays. Children with autism have significant language delays. Up to fifty percent of children with autism never speak. Those who do develop language have trouble carrying on conversations. They may say the same things over and over. Children with autism don't usually use or respond to nonverbal communications such as eye contact, facial expressions, or gestures.

Repetitive behaviors. Children with autism tend to repeat certain behaviors again and again. They may line up toy cars or stare at a ceiling fan. They may move their bodies in unusual ways, such as flapping their hands or rocking back and forth on their feet. Children with autism like rituals and routines and get very upset if these routines are interrupted or cut short.

Other symptoms. Many children diagnosed with autism also have sensory difficulties and may seem unaware of sensory stimulation. For example, a child may not notice that the shirt he's wearing is soaking wet. But children with autism can also be overly sensitive. For example, they may get very upset if they get paint on their fingers. They may have cognitive delays and fail to develop personal care skills as expected. Children with autism have a higher than normal rate of seizure disorders.

CAUSES

The exact cause of autism is unknown, though researchers suspect a genetic link. Studies have shown differences in the brain structure of some children with autism. Autism is not caused by poor parenting.

TREATMENT

Early intervention is important. A child with autism needs the expertise of many specialists. Speech therapy is needed for communication delays. Physical and occupational therapy is needed for sensory problems (over- and under-sensitivities) and for development of personal care skills. Getting the support of a mental health professional is often recommended for both the child and the family. Both primary and secondary caregivers need to learn about autism and understand what can be done at home and in child care settings to support the child's development, including what expectations and discipline are appropriate. The child may need individual and/or group-based intervention to help him learn to relate to others. Psychological interventions such as "Floor Time," developed by Stanley Greenspan, MD, or Relationship Development Intervention (RDI), developed by Steven Gutstein, PhD, can teach caregivers how to help the child learn to interact with others, expand his interests, become more flexible regarding changes in routines, and develop problem-solving skills.

Medications are often used as a way to help manage severe symptoms, such as aggression, self-injury, and tantrums. Some clinicians recommend additional interventions, such as vitamins, dietary supplements, and other more-experimental approaches, though these interventions have not been well studied.

CLASSROOM AND CHILD CARE SETTING STRATEGIES

Stay in communication with caregivers. Children improve most when all of their adult caregivers work together as a united team. Children with autism require consistency, and they need to know that all the adults in their life are in regular communication. For suggestions about establishing and maintaining communication with caregivers, see chapter 4. Help parents understand your concerns and encourage them to seek evaluation for their child. Accurate diagnosis and early intervention are very important. Share with parents your exact concerns, rather than trying to make a diagnosis or suggesting the child has autism or Asperger's. For example, say, "Jenny should be talking more. She keeps to herself all the time, and I can't get her to stop playing with the beads." The parents may respond by saying that they see similar behaviors at home, but they may be unaware that their child is not developing as expected.

Discussing your concerns with the family may be a sensitive and long-term process. Most families are reluctant to think that their child might have a diagnosis such as autism. Because it is a diagnosis that can be extremely painful and difficult to accept, most families go through a period of guilt, mourning, and adjustment once this diagnosis is made.

Once the diagnosis is made, try to be involved with the treatment team and intervention process as much as possible. Children who are in a full-day program, in particular, need your active engagement in the process. Work together with the team to develop strategies for use in the classroom or child care setting that are specific to the child.

Focus on the development of the child's social skills. Provide the child with a small group setting and with as much one-on-one interaction as possible.

Provide a structured environment with clear and consistent limits and routines. Providing the child with regular routines will help him learn what is expected. Develop specific routines, especially for transition times. Changes and lack of routine can easily trigger overstimulation and tantrums.

Encourage the child to communicate. For example, require the child to make a gesture or sound or to say a word before you give her something. Use language with the child constantly. Repeat back anything she says. Give her choices that require a verbal response. Say, for example, "Would you like the red paint or the blue paint?" Use positive reinforcement when the child does try to communicate.

Encourage and help the child interact with others. You can start with something as simple as getting the child to make eye contact. Put a desired object near your face or eyes, so the child has to make eye contact before he can get it. Encourage the child to do any activity that requires some give-and-take, such as rolling a ball back and forth.

If the child shows signs of sensory sensitivity or sensory seeking, provide appropriate interventions. For more details, refer to the classroom and child care setting strategies section regarding regulatory disorders in chapter 6.

Build on the child's interests. Set aside a short period of time each day to play with the child one-on-one. Follow his lead in play until he feels comfortable and safe with you being there, even if that means nothing but lining up the cars with him for a period of time. You'll be building the foundation of shared interaction. Then add small things to the play to expand his interests. For example, move the cars differently or add sounds or other toys. Encourage the child to hand the car back and forth for short periods.

Asperger's Disorder

Five-year-old Carlos talks endlessly about trains. Rather than play with kids his age, he likes to talk with adults, who politely listen to his monologues. He doesn't know how to enter play or how to chat with another child. Children avoid playing with him because he always wants to do the same thing and he doesn't seem to notice their suggestions. Unless people speak very directly and concretely, Carlos doesn't seem to understand what people are trying to tell him. He likes his own routines and sense of order and gets upset if others try to change or interrupt him. Carlos knows that he's different, but he wants to have friends. He just doesn't seem able to figure out how anyone does that.

TYPICAL SYMPTOMS

Mental health professionals disagree about whether Asperger's disorder is different from autism or is a form of high-functioning autism. The diagnostic criteria for Asperger's disorder are similar to those for autism, with some important differences (adapted from the DSM-IV-TR):

- Like children with autism, children with Asperger's disorder have trouble with social interactions. They have a hard time reading body language or learning how to enter play or join a group. But, unlike children with autism, children with Asperger's are interested in others and want to figure out how to have friends.

- Children with Asperger's disorder usually don't have communication delays. Their vocabulary and grammar are typical for children their age. In fact, children with Asperger's tend to talk quite a bit. However, their communications tend to be one-sided. They don't usually have back-and-forth conversations. Rather, they ramble on about topics they're interested in without realizing that others have lost interest or are ready to end the conversation.

- Like children with autism, children with Asperger's disorder develop highly specific interests and prefer routines and rituals. They are, however, more likely than children with autism to want to share those interests with others.

- Like children with autism, children with Asperger's disorder may have sensory integration difficulties.

- Children with Asperger's disorder usually don't have delays in cognitive development or personal care skills. In fact, many children with Asperger's have areas of intellectual giftedness.

TREATMENT

Early intervention for Asperger's disorder is important, and the child may need multiple therapies. Speech therapy can help children with this disorder learn how to talk with others. They need coaching, instruction, and practice to learn conversation turn-taking and how to read body language. Physical and occupational therapy may be needed if the child has sensory problems or poor coordination. A mental health professional is a helpful ally for both the child and the family. Caregivers need to learn about Asperger's disorder so they can understand what can be done at home to support the child's development. To address social skills and emotion regulation, children with this disorder often need individual and/or group-based intervention.

CLASSROOM AND CHILD CARE SETTING STRATEGIES

Stay in communication with caregivers. Children improve most when all of their adult caregivers work together as a united team. Children with Asperger's disorder require consistency, and they need to know that all the adults in their life are in regular communication. For suggestions about establishing and maintaining communication with caregivers, see chapter 4.

Provide both opportunities for and help with social interactions. Teach the child the basics of how to enter and exit play, take turns, and listen to input from others. Children with Asperger's need help learning how to understand the perspectives of others, and they need to learn the unspoken rules of interactions. For example, they need to learn how close to stand near people, when it's okay to touch others, and how to notice when other children are communicating that they're done talking or playing with them. Your teaching will be most effective if it is done in a concrete and simple step-by-step manner. You can include these lessons in circle time as part of your ongoing promotion of social skills in the classroom or child care setting. A child with Asperger's also may need some one-on-one intervention at key times, such as during free play. Set aside time to be near the child during highly social times and provide verbal instructions and support during interactions.

Like children with autism, children with Asperger's benefit from small group settings, individualized attention, and clear and consistent routines and expectations.

If the child is showing signs of sensory sensitivity or is sensory seeking, provide appropriate interventions. For more details, refer to the classroom and child care setting strategies section on regulatory disorders in chapter 6.

CHAPTER 11: Sleeping, Eating, and Elimination Disorders

I n the normal development stages of infancy through the preschool years, children are expected to learn to regulate their sleeping and waking cycles and their eating patterns. For example, they should know when they are hungry and when they are full, and they should begin to sleep through the night. In time, they are also expected to successfully complete toilet learning.

Without taking into account cultural expectations, it's hard to define at what age to expect children to fall asleep on their own or to stay dry during the day. Some families expect a child to be tidy and responsible about toileting at a very early age, while others wait for children to teach themselves. In many cultures, children sleep with their caregivers. Some families wouldn't think of putting a baby to sleep in her own bed until she's at least three years old. In other families, an infant is kept in a cradle in her own room before she's a month old.

Even accounting for differing cultural norms, children tend to develop along their own timetables. A full-term infant may sleep through the night at two months old, while a premature baby might still be waking for night feedings at six months. One baby may love to eat cereal from the first day it's offered, while another may spit out solid foods for a few months longer. One child can't wait to sit on the potty, while another can't be bothered. These are all variations of normal development.

However, not all children meet normal expectations for developing the skills to regulate their eating, sleeping, and elimination behaviors. Some experience disorders that delay development in one or more of these areas.

SLEEPING DISORDERS

For the past two weeks, four-year-old Alejandro has been waking up in the middle of his nap screaming and crying. He talks about monsters and other scary things and wants to be held and reassured. Alejandro has become so afraid that he doesn't want to go down for his nap. He runs around the classroom and gets into trouble in order to avoid having to lie down and fall asleep. He looks exhausted every day and he is becoming more irritable and fussy all the time.

TYPICAL SYMPTOMS

Most children develop regular sleep patterns by the time they're a year old. Before that age, a sleep disorder diagnosis would be unusual. Psychologists have identified many different kinds of sleep disorders, each with unique symptoms. The following diagnoses and accompanying symptoms were adapted from the DSM-IV-TR and the DC:0–3R.

Sleep terror disorder. The child gets up a number of times at night screaming with fear. She may be sweating and her heart may be pounding. Although she is "up," she's not really awake. It's often hard to soothe a child during a terror episode. When awake, the child doesn't remember having the nightmare.

Nightmare disorder. The child often wakes from nightmares. Unlike the child with night terrors, this child can remember the frightening dreams, which usually involve threats to safety or survival. The child is alert after waking from the nightmare and usually responds well to soothing activities.

Sleepwalking disorder. The child gets up at night, gets out of bed, and walks around. Again, this child is "up" but not fully awake. The child often doesn't respond to anyone and doesn't remember the event the next morning.

Breathing-related sleep disorder. The child has trouble staying asleep because he's having difficulty breathing. Sleep apnea is one cause of this disorder. Another cause may be a medical problem that involves significantly shallow or slow breathing or significantly lower levels of oxygen and/or carbon dioxide, such as severe asthma. The child is usually very tired and lacks energy because he isn't getting enough deep sleep.

Sleeping, Eating, and Elimination Disorders Symptoms at a Glance

Sleeping disorders	Eating disorders	Elimination disorders
• difficulty falling asleep • can't fall asleep alone • frequently wakes up • frequently goes to caregiver's bed in the middle of the night • nightmares • night terrors • sleepwalks	• doesn't eat enough to grow • loses weight • lacks interest in food • upset at mealtimes • overly picky about foods	• urinates or has bowel movements in inappropriate places or at inappropriate times (must be at least four years old for bowel movement difficulties and at least five years old for urination difficulties)

Other difficulties or characteristics that resemble sleeping, eating, or elimination disorders include:

• problems in the primary attachment relationship
• medical difficulties
• side effects of medications

Sleeping, eating, and elimination difficulties also are frequently found as symptoms for other disorders. For example:

• Children with mood or anxiety disorders often have problems sleeping and eating.
• Difficulty falling asleep and food aversion are common in regulatory disorders.
• Nightmares and night terrors are common in posttraumatic stress disorder (PTSD) and bipolar disorder.
• Toileting accidents (elimination problems) are often seen in children with PTSD who are taking a step back in development or in children who have been physically or sexually abused.
• Children with regulatory disorders or childhood-onset schizophrenia may display inappropriate toilet behaviors.

Sleep-onset disorder. The child has trouble falling asleep. She often needs somebody to stay with her. If nobody stays in the room, she'll probably call someone in many times before she finally falls asleep. To be diagnosed with this disorder, the problem has to happen at least five nights a week for four weeks.

Night-waking disorder. The child wakes at night calling for somebody to come into his room. Either someone has to stay in the room with the child or the child needs to get into his parents' bed in order to fall back asleep. To be diagnosed with this disorder, the problem has to happen at least five nights a week for four weeks.

CAUSES

The exact cause of many of these disorders is unknown, but research has suggested the following:

- Sleep terror disorder and sleepwalking disorder seem to run in families, which suggests a possible genetic link.

- Night terror disorder is common in children who have bipolar disorder, but other children may have night terrors as well.

- Nightmare disorder is more common in children who have experienced severe trauma or stress. Children who have not been traumatized may also have nightmares.

- Sleep-onset disorder and night-waking disorder are often related to parenting practices and expectations about sleeping.

TREATMENT

Ways to help a child with a sleep disorder vary depending on the type of disorder.

Night terror disorder and sleepwalking disorder. Treatment often focuses on helping the child reduce stress and anxiety, especially right before bedtime. Strategies might include establishing regular bedtime routines, avoiding scary videos, and avoiding shouting or fighting in the evening. If necessary, medications that reduce depression and anxiety are sometimes considered.

Nightmare disorder. Because this disorder often is the result of trauma or stress, the child and her family often need both individual and family therapy.

Medications may be prescribed to reduce associated anxiety, depression, or related difficulties.

Sleep-onset and night-waking disorders. These disorders often respond well to changes in caregiving practices. Caregiver education and possibly caregiver therapy might be needed. Making these changes often is difficult for caregivers. They need a great deal of support and encouragement to follow through.

CLASSROOM AND CHILD CARE SETTING STRATEGIES

Stay in communication with caregivers. Children improve most when all of their adult caregivers work together as a united team. Children with sleeping disorders require consistency, and they need to know that all the adults in their life are in regular communication. For suggestions about establishing and maintaining communication with caregivers, see chapter 4.

Be consistent with naptime. Start the child's naptime routine at the same time every day. Do the same things in the same order every time. For example, first change his diaper and take off his shoes, and then wash his hands, settle him on the mat, and tuck him in. Maintain the same environment from the time he lies down until he wakes up. For example, if you play music for the child to fall asleep, leave the music on until he wakes up. If you have a light on as the child falls asleep, leave it on until he wakes up. Don't have loud conversations or make loud noises during naptime. Keep the bedding and room temperature comfortable.

Help children relax. Sometimes a child with a sleeping disorder may need extra attention. Hold or rock the child, rub her back, stroke her hair, or sit nearby to help settle her down. Some children respond well to singing or to soft, reassuring talk. You might say, "You're safe here. I will be here the whole time. It's okay to fall asleep." Don't allow the child to fall completely asleep in your arms. Instead, once she's relaxed and nodding off, move her to her crib, mat, or cot. That way she can take her final sleep steps on her own. When you hold a child until she's fully asleep, you teach her to rely on you to take those final sleep steps for her.

Respect individual needs for sleep. Although most children need a quiet time during the day, some children do not need to sleep. This is especially true for children who are getting ready to move on to kindergarten. Let the child know that he can lie down quietly or read a book by himself if he doesn't want to nap.

EATING DISORDERS

Rhonda, who is five years old, has always been very skinny, but lately she seems to be losing weight. She never seems to be hungry, and she barely touches the food on her plate. Even when the provider encourages her and offers her tasty foods and treats, she shows no interest. Her mother has noticed this at home too, and says she'll take Rhonda to the doctor soon.

TYPICAL SYMPTOMS

The following diagnoses and accompanying symptoms have been adapted from the DSM-IV-TR and the DC:0–3R.

Pica. A child with pica eats things that aren't food, such as paint, plaster, string, hair, cloth, animal droppings, leaves, insects, sand, or pebbles. For behavior to be diagnosed as a disorder,

- the child has to exhibit this unusual eating pattern often over the course of one month or more and

- the eating needs to be unusual for the child's developmental age. Eating things that aren't food is common in children under eighteen months. This diagnosis is considered for children this young only if the behavior is severe.

Rumination disorder. A child with rumination disorder throws up and rechews her food over a period of one month or more. To be diagnosed as a disorder, this behavior cannot be caused by a physical problem such as reflux.

Feeding disorder of infancy or early childhood. The child doesn't eat enough to grow and gain weight as expected, even though she's offered enough food. She may even lose weight. To be diagnosed as a disorder, the problem cannot be caused by a medical problem such as reflux or cleft palette.

Feeding disorder of state regulation. The infant does not get enough food because she's unable to remain calm and concentrate during feeding times. She may be too sleepy to nurse, or too agitated and distressed. To be diagnosed as a disorder, the problem must have started when the child was a newborn, and she must have lost weight or failed to gain weight as expected.

Feeding disorder of caregiver-infant reciprocity. The child does not engage with his caregiver during feeding times. Unlike typical babies, he doesn't make eye contact, smile, or babble during feedings. To be diagnosed with this disorder, the child must fail to gain weight as expected, and his lack of engagement cannot be caused by another issue such as vision impairment or autism.

Infantile anorexia. The child refuses to eat adequate amounts of food. She doesn't seem interested in food and doesn't say she's hungry. To be diagnosed as a disorder,

- the problem has to begin before the child is three years old,
- the problem must last for at least a month,
- the child must fail to gain weight as expected, and
- the problem cannot be the result of another medical condition or trauma.

Sensory food aversion. The child refuses to eat certain foods with specific tastes, textures, or smells. She won't eat new foods but does eat familiar favorite foods. To be diagnosed as a disorder, the eating problem has to give the child some kind of nutritional deficiency or cause a delay in oral-motor development.

Feeding disorder associated with concurrent medical condition. The child is interested in eating but gets distressed during the meal and refuses to keep eating, even though he may still be hungry. To be diagnosed as a disorder,

- the child must also have a diagnosed medical condition, such as acid reflux, that makes it stressful for him to eat,
- the problem has to continue even when the medical condition is being addressed, and
- the child must also lose weight or fail to gain weight as expected.

Feeding disorder associated with insults to the gastrointestinal tract. The child ate well until she had a bad experience with her mouth, throat, stomach, or intestinal tract. For example, the child may have choked on a grape, had severe vomiting, or had her stomach pumped. To be diagnosed with this disorder,

- the child must refuse all feeding or certain types of feedings,

- the child must get upset either at reminders of the trauma, such as seeing grapes, or when she sees food being set out for her, and

- the problem must be a threat to the child's health.

You may also hear of a condition called failure to thrive, or FTT. FTT is not a specific diagnosis in either the DSM-IV-TR or the DC:0–3R, so a detailed description is not included in this chapter. FTT is a category that includes children who are below the fifth percentile in weight for their age and children who have had a significant drop in weight (for example, weight for age drops across two major percentile lines on a growth chart). The causes of FTT can be very narrow, such as a specific medical problem, but most often FTT results from a complex combination of medical problems, developmental delays, difficulties in the caregiver-child relationship, and family stress.

CAUSES

Although the exact cause of many of these disorders is unknown, research has shown that:

- Pica and rumination disorder are relatively rare. They are usually related to developmental delays such as mental retardation and autism.

- Feeding disorder associated with concurrent medical condition and feeding disorder associated with insults to the gastrointestinal tract are triggered by medical conditions and/or trauma.

- Feeding disorder of state regulation and sensory food aversion are commonly seen in children with regulatory disorders.

- Feeding disorder of caregiver-infant reciprocity seems to be highly related to the bond between the caregiver and the infant.

TREATMENT

Intervention varies depending on the specific type of disorder:

- Rumination disorder often fades away on its own.

- Pica is often treated as part of a larger treatment plan that addresses the child's other developmental needs.

- When children have sensory food aversions, therapists work with the family to find ways to make food more appealing to the child. Some children will eat food if it's blended to a smooth consistency. Other children do better with cut-up raw fruits and vegetables, instead of soft, cooked foods. The therapist and caregivers can also work together to find ways to slowly introduce new foods and textures. Vitamins may be helpful if the child will take them.

- When children don't eat because of medical problems, both medical and mental health specialists are needed to help the child. While doctors treat the medical condition, therapists support the family to work through their fears about their child's disorder and to encourage the child to enjoy eating again.

- For children who aren't eating because of a trauma, treatment usually focuses both on the trauma itself and on the child's fears and emotions around food.

CLASSROOM AND CHILD CARE SETTING STRATEGIES

Stay in communication with caregivers. Children improve most when all of their adult caregivers work together as a united team. Children with eating disorders require consistency, and they need to know that all the adults in their life are in regular communication. For suggestions about establishing and maintaining communication with caregivers, see chapter 4.

Find out what the family knows about the child's eating problems. You may need to respond differently to a child who has had his stomach pumped than to a child who gags at lumpy foods due to sensory sensitivity.

Talk to caregivers about what they do at home and what has been successful. Does the child do better with soft foods or small bites? Share with caregivers the strategies that have worked at school. Does the child do better when she serves herself family-style? Is the child more willing to eat food she makes herself during a cooking project?

Provide attractive foods and be willing to consider alternatives for children who are struggling with food refusal. For example, if a child eats only soft foods, let him have a second helping of apple sauce even if he hasn't finished his crackers.

Avoid battles about eating. Don't force children or make a big deal out of eating. Power struggles often make matters worse.

Elimination Disorders

Five-year-old Jacob seems angry and is aggressive with the other children. He has high energy and has a lot of difficulty paying attention in class. Jacob refuses to nap and needs a great deal of supervision to follow the classroom routine. The provider has talked to his mother about these concerns before, but his mother has not yet taken him in for an evaluation. Things don't seem to be getting any better, and in the past few months, Jacob has soiled his pants several times. He seems embarrassed and often doesn't mention it for a while. He says he didn't mean to do it and can't say why it happened. He's reluctant to help with cleaning up the mess. The provider is becoming more and more convinced that Jacob needs help in several areas and that the soiling accidents are part of a larger picture.

TYPICAL SYMPTOMS

The DSM-IV-TR criteria for wetting problems (enuresis) include:

- The child wets the bed or his clothes (whether voluntarily or intentionally) at least twice a week for three consecutive months.

- The wetting accidents cause significant distress or impairment.

- The child is at least five years old.

- The accidents are unrelated to a medical condition.

The DSM-IV-TR criteria for soiling problems (encopresis) include:

- The child repeatedly has bowel movements in inappropriate places (for example, in her clothing or on the floor).

- These inappropriate bowel movements occur at least once a month for three consecutive months.

- The child is at least four years old.

- The accidents are unrelated to a medical condition.

CAUSES

The exact cause of these disorders is unknown, but some common factors are:

Wetting

- A history of wetting tends to run in families, suggesting it may be hereditary.

- Wetting is sometimes associated with other developmental delays; with delays in or lack of appropriate toilet training; and with stress.

- Anxiety about toileting, or toileting in new and different places, can lead a child to try to "hold it in," and she may then have an accident.

- Traumatic experiences can lead a child to take a step backward in her toilet learning.

- Children who have been sexually abused may have difficulties with toileting.

Soiling

- Many children suffering from soiling have a history of constipation. Prolonged constipation can make bowel movements painful, so a child may try to hold it in as long as possible, which can lead to leakage and, ultimately, to a soiling accident.

- The embarrassment and anxiety associated with soiling can make the problem worse; the child may begin to feel worried about toileting successfully or develop a fear of the bathroom.

- Many children with soiling problems have a history of delayed, poor, or inconsistent toilet training.

- Significant stress, change, trauma, and/or abuse can lead to difficulties with soiling.

- Purposely having a bowel movement in inappropriate places or smearing a stool is often a child's way of attempting to gain control over a difficult aspect of his life. In this case, the soiling problem must be considered in a larger context.

TREATMENT

Wetting usually decreases gradually with age. Because children with wetting problems are often embarrassed and ashamed, warm support and understanding are very important. Treatment, which is rarely recommended before age six, may include:

- Use of a bedwetting alarm, which rings the moment a sensor detects wetness on the bed. The alarm helps the child wake up to go to the bathroom. Most children need six to eight weeks of alarm training before they can wake themselves up to go to the bathroom.

- For children who wet during the day, frequent reminders and bathroom scheduling can be helpful.

- Medications such as tricyclic antidepressants or desmopressin (DDAVP) often can successfully treat the symptoms of wetting, but they may not be suitable for all ages.

The treatment of soiling often involves both medical and psychological intervention:

- Often the child will need to empty his blocked intestinal tract through the use of laxatives or enemas. A proper diet with good amounts of fluids and fiber will help support intestinal movement and prevent constipation.

- Children with soiling problems often benefit from a defined toileting routine and ongoing use of mild laxatives.

- Warm support and understanding, as well as nonjudgmental communication about toileting, are very important.

- If soiling is a result of trauma, stress, or other emotional difficulties, the treatment may be more complex and must address the underlying factors in order to be successful.

CLASSROOM AND CHILD CARE SETTING STRATEGIES

Stay in communication with caregivers. Children improve most when all of their adult caregivers work together as a united team. Children with elimination disorders require consistency, and they need to know that all the adults in their life are in regular communication. For suggestions about establishing and maintaining communication with caregivers, see chapter 4.

Recommend a medical evaluation if the child has not had one already. The problem may be caused by a medical condition, such as a urinary tract infection or constipation. Toileting problems can also be a side effect of some medications.

Make toileting a comfortable topic in the classroom or child care setting. Include picture books about toileting, such as *Everyone Poops, The Story of the Little Mole Who Went in Search of Whodunit,* and *I Have to Go!*

Don't scold or criticize a child when she has a toileting accident. She is likely to be embarrassed and ashamed enough already. Treat the incident in a matter-of-fact manner. Be supportive as you help the child get cleaned up. Don't force the child to clean urine or feces off the floor.

Help the child become more aware of his need to use the bathroom. Check in with the child from time to time to see if he needs to go.

Set up a schedule or times for just sitting and trying. This might be very effective if accidents seem to happen at specific times such as naptime or outside time.

Help the child feel comfortable in the bathroom. Some children do better with more privacy. Others may do better if the teacher or provider stays with them in the bathroom. Many children are most comfortable if their feet can remain flat on the floor while they're on the toilet. If the toilet is too high for this, provide a stepstool on which children can rest their feet.

Avoid battles about toileting. Contention is likely to make things worse.

CHAPTER 12: Childhood-Onset Schizophrenia

Schizophrenia is a serious mental illness that usually starts sometime between the late teens and the early thirties. Rarely, children as young as five or six show signs of schizophrenia (DSM-IV-TR). Schizophrenia before the age of thirteen is called childhood-onset schizophrenia.

Teachers can't quite figure out four-year-old Luo. He seems to have a good vocabulary and uses full sentences, but for some reason they have a hard time making sense of what he's saying. When teachers ask him questions to help them understand, his answers don't make sense. Luo often seems confused and struggles to complete tasks that have more than one step. Although he's generally a sweet boy, he sometimes becomes aggressive out of the blue. For example, he'll be sitting quietly and then suddenly hit the child next to him with a toy. Luo likes to play by himself. Teachers say he sometimes giggles to himself as if someone has just told him a joke. The teachers don't quite know what to say when he points to the corner of the room and talks about the dinosaur he sees there. They don't know if he's being creative and imaginative or if he really thinks he sees one. On a few occasions, teachers have been flustered when Luo does something they find highly unusual. For example, even though he's known how to use the bathroom for a long time, Luo once pulled down his pants and defecated under the jungle gym.

Childhood-Onset Schizophrenia Symptoms at a Glance

- seems to see or hear things that are not actually there
- has strange ideas that cannot be true
- child's speech is difficult to understand because of frequent topic changes or because what he's saying doesn't make sense
- has difficulty organizing his behavior to complete a task
- exhibits bizarre behaviors
- is unresponsive and/or withdrawn

Other difficulties that resemble childhood-onset schizophrenia disorders include the following:

- problems in the primary attachment relationship
- bipolar disorder
- autism
- posttraumatic stress disorder

TYPICAL SYMPTOMS

The DSM-IV-TR criteria for diagnosing schizophrenia are the same for both children and adults. However, since very young children may not have all the symptoms of schizophrenia, a diagnosis of this disorder may not be made until a child is older. Early signs of schizophrenia in children may differ from those in adults. For example, the symptoms of disorganized speech and behavior are more common in young children with early signs of schizophrenia. Young children may have hallucinations and delusions that are not as detailed and organized as the ones adults experience (Clark and Lewis 1998). Children are also more likely to have visual hallucinations than are adults. Children diagnosed with childhood-onset schizophrenia often have motor, language, and social-skill delays and may be very withdrawn from others.

The child must have two or more of the following symptoms most of the time for at least a month to meet DSM-IV-TR criteria for schizophrenia. Also, the child must have some evidence of symptoms for at least six full months, even if all the criteria are not met for that longer time period. Typical symptoms (adapted from the DSM-IV-TR) include:

- Delusions

- Hallucinations

- Disorganized speech

- Highly disorganized behavior. The child may have difficulty paying attention, following directions, and completing tasks.

- Strange and inappropriate behavior, including unusually silly or strange movements that seem odd for a child, such as wriggling on the floor for no apparent reason. Of course, all children do silly things. The important difference is that this bizarre type of silliness happens a lot, along with other symptoms. Older children may have inappropriate sexual behaviors.

- Little interest in or awareness of personal hygiene

- May be withdrawn, unresponsive to others, or fail to show any emotion

Delusions are unusual ideas that have no basis in reality, yet the child believes these things are really true. For example, a child might complain that people are staring at her all the time, even though they're not. Or she may say that someone is trying to hurt her, even when no children are playing near her or even paying any attention to her. Delusions tend to be scary, and the child may believe them strongly, even when presented with contradictory evidence. Of course, one's personal experiences and cultural beliefs must be taken into account when considering whether a child's beliefs are truly delusional. For example, if a child talks about seeing spirits, this experience may be delusional or it may simply reflect the child's particular cultural or religious understanding. Checking out the child's statement with her family will help clarify whether this belief is unusual.

Hallucinations are sensory experiences of things that aren't really there. The child may hear voices or see things that nobody else sees or hears. Even though these things are not really happening, they seem very real to the child. Hallucinations that involve the sense of smell, taste, or touch are less common.

Disorganized speech refers to when a child makes no sense when he talks, even though he's using real words and real sentences. His thoughts may jump around and he may make no connection between topics. For example, if you ask the child about a recent trip to Disneyland, he might answer, "I went to Disneyland. And then the dinosaur came and my milk got blue all over and my birthday is tomorrow." Talk like this is sometimes called "word salad."

CAUSES

Schizophrenia is probably caused by a combination of genetics and environment. Research shows that the brains of people with schizophrenia look different from the brains of people without the disorder. Also, children with a close relative who has been diagnosed with schizophrenia have a tenfold higher risk of developing the disorder (DSM-IV-TR; Gonthier and Lyon 2004).

Trauma, a poor relationship with a primary caregiver, harsh parenting, poverty, and family stress can make schizophrenia worse and more difficult to manage. When individuals with schizophrenia leave treatment centers and return to caregivers who are harsh, critical, or confusing, they are more likely to relapse and have to return to the hospital (Dulmus and Smyth 2000).

TREATMENT

Children should be diagnosed and treated as early as possible. Early treatment helps them participate in school and be in social relationships along with other children. With early treatment, children may be able to avoid being hospitalized or may be hospitalized fewer times. A child with schizophrenia usually is given antipsychotic medication. She may need to take this medication for the rest of her life.

Therapy for the child and the family is often very helpful. Caregivers need help and support to understand the disorder. They need to learn how to respond appropriately to the child and they need to learn effective strategies for caring for the child. Therapy can help children learn appropriate social skills and techniques for soothing themselves before they spin out of control. Learning about emotions is also helpful for these children.

CLASSROOM AND CHILD CARE SETTING STRATEGIES

Stay in communication with caregivers. Children improve most when all of their adult caregivers work together as a united team. Children with schizophrenia require consistency, and they need to know that all the adults in their life are in regular communication. For suggestions about establishing and maintaining communication with caregivers, see chapter 4. As a provider, you may be one of the first people to notice unusual behavior. Hearing your observations can be scary for parents. Be clear with them about what you observe and why you are concerned. As always, don't attempt to make a diagnosis and avoid words such as "delusions" or "schizophrenia." Ask parents what kinds of behaviors they notice with their child at home. Encourage families to seek professional evaluation. Remind them that the sooner problems are identified, the sooner the child can get the help he needs to live a happy and successful life. Remember that even when a child gets evaluated, she may not have enough symptoms to be diagnosed with schizophrenia. A diagnosis may have to wait until she is older, when more symptoms may be observable.

Work to build a close and trusting relationship. This may not be easy. You may even feel like avoiding the child, because communicating with him takes a lot of work. You may end up feeling like you're talking to yourself. Continue to look for opportunities to connect. If the child likes to play alone at the water table, for example, try to join in and play side by side with him. Maybe he'll allow you to rub his back at rest time, or perhaps he'll help you set the table for lunch. Take advantage of any opportunity you can find to engage with the child in a warm and affectionate way.

Help the child learn about and feel safe with her emotions. Use active listening to validate the child's feelings. For example, if the child says, "I'm scared the lights will eat me," you might say, "I can see you're scared. Come with me. I'll keep you safe while we look at the lights. Let's see what they're all about."

Help the child learn social and emotional skills such as give-and-take play and give-and-take conversation. Teach the child these skills the same way you teach numbers or shapes. Model, coach, practice, and role-play.

Draw ideas from the classroom and child care setting strategies listed for ADHD, ODD, and conduct disorder as well as those listed for bipolar disorder. Some of these strategies also can be helpful for children with symptoms of schizophrenia. Try some of the suggestions for reducing stimulation, establishing consistent routines, providing structure, recognizing positive behaviors, teaching social skills, handling aggression, and working with tantrums.

APPENDIX A
Social/Emotional Developmental Continuum

	Infant	Young Toddler	Older Toddler	Preschooler	Pre-kindergartener
Seeks trusted adults for companion-ship, affec-tion, comfort, and support	Looks into adult eyes during nursing or bottle feeding. Responds to adult soothing. Recognizes and reaches out to familiar adults.	Seeks to remain near familiar adults. Returns to familiar adults for comfort, for help, and to participate in simple games. Shows distress around unfamiliar people. Imitates actions of familiar people.	Requests adult help and attention. Begins to participate in caregiving routines and simple games. Uses a transitional object to symbolically keep adult close. Alternates between clinging to and resisting adult.	Looks to adults as resources and role models. Can separate from adult without distress.	Enjoys working and playing with adults. Seeks adult help and support when needed.
Examples	Stops crying when picked up and rocked by adult. Holds arms out to mother at the end of the day.	Crawls to follow adult around room. Goes back and forth between exploring environment and sitting on adult's lap. Plays peek-a-boo with adult. Turns head away from visitor. Tries to take sunglasses from adult and put on own face.	Calls "Help me" when trying to climb onto a high stool. Wipes face with paper towel given by adult after meal. Plays chase game with adult. Carries blankie or photo of family around as comfort item during stressful times. Pulls away and says, "No" one moment, then runs back for hugs and affection the next.	Mimics family members in home living center. Asks to help provider push snack cart back to kitchen. Kisses provider's finger when hurt in the door. Hugs Daddy good-bye in the morning and goes off to find playmate.	Comes over to help provider move tables over for dancing activity. Asks provider to fetch more blue paint for project. Asks provider to play Candy Land with him. Comes to provider for bandage when hurt in play yard.

	Infant	Young Toddler	Older Toddler	Preschooler	Pre-kindergartener
Looks to others for companionship, connection, and community	Searches for faces. Explores faces and bodies of others. Watches and responds to other children. Is interested in being with others.	Shows interest in other children at play. Participates in sustained play near other children with minimal interactions.	Seeks company during play. Plays with one or two favored children. For a short time, sustains play with another child with common themes. Begins to participate in routines with other children.	Enters ongoing play with one or more children, integrating easily into the play. Engages in social games and pretend play with others.	Identifies a child as a best friend and is identified in return. Leads or participates in coordinated play with others. Identifies self as a member of a group.
Examples	Turns head to follow movements of older child. Reaches out to touch face of nearby baby.	Watches children crawling up loft steps. Plays fill and dump game next to a child looking at a book.	Goes to block and car area where others are playing. "Drives" cars with special buddy most days at choice time. Runs to join activity table when sees provider take out a cooking project.	Watches children making rivers in sand and begins to help. Goes to children at the sensory table and asks, "What are you doing?" Pretends to be the pet cat in the home living area.	"I'll be the mommy and you be the baby." Builds a big city with others in the construction area. "I'm a sunshine kid."

	Infant	Young Toddler	Older Toddler	Preschooler	Pre-kindergartener
Learns to regulate behavior, emotions, and attention	Develops eating and sleeping patterns. Shows emotions with body. Begins to find strategies to self-soothe. Responds to attempts of adults to soothe her. Begins to show interest in sights and sounds.	Uses adults to co-regulate. Uses transitional objects to manage separation. Comforts self by seeking a specific person or special object. Gets involved, but is easily distracted.	Toilet learning. Follows simple routines with reminders. Responds to and tests limits. Gets distracted but returns to task.	Follows established routines. Can adjust behavior based on setting and situation. Regulates behavior with self-talk. Relies on adult structured processes for turn taking, waiting, and sharing. Can concentrate on a task.	Anticipates and participates in daily routines, transitions, and activities. Accepts changes in daily routines and schedules. Can regulate own behavior/emotions/attention using learned techniques. Identifies emotional triggers for self and others. Can do two things at once.
Examples	Settles into two naps a day, one in the morning and one after lunch. Cries and curls up arms and legs when hungry. Sucks fingers to relax into sleep. Stops crying when rocked by an adult. Watches mobile move in the wind. Turns head to voices.	Reaches for object and looks at adult for approval before continuing on. Carries Tata's purse around when she misses home. Plays with toy drum but drops it immediately when he sees another interesting activity.	Begins toilet learning. With adult reminder, washes hands before snack. Runs away when called to come inside. Looks up from water table when hears kids laughing, but returns to his play.	Runs outside, but, with reminders, walks in the hallway. Says to self, "Flush the toilet," after using bathroom. With adult prompting, lets another child have a turn on the swing. Continues to work on art project even when other activities are going on around her.	Comes in from outdoor time and sits right down in the circle area for story time without prompting. Manages field trip to library without falling apart. Takes turns, shares, waits, and "uses words" if previously taught and modeled by others. Says, "LaHana is crying because nobody will give her a turn." Can eat lunch and carry on conversation at the same time.

	Infant	Young Toddler	Older Toddler	Preschooler	Pre-kindergartener
Develops communication and social skills to interact with others	Smiles and makes sounds of pleasure when others are around. Cries to communicate needs. Responds to social play with babbling.	Follows one-step instructions for familiar tasks. Expresses basic needs, wants, and feelings through simple actions and crying. Understands simple words and phrases.	Uses basic language to attempt to communicate with others. Begins symbolic play. Uses physical behavior when he lacks social language.	Follows two-step instructions for familiar tasks. Uses language in more sophisticated ways to describe feelings and to tell a story with a beginning, middle, and end.	Follows three-step instructions for unfamiliar tasks. Understands "how" and "why" language. Can describe feelings and what caused them (emotional cause and effect). Has extended conversations sharing emotions, ideas, and information.
Examples	Smiles in response to adult smile. Cries when diaper is soiled. Babbles back in response to somebody talking or playing with her.	Waves bye-bye when prompted. Holds up cup to get more milk. Cries or fusses when hungry or overtired. Holds arms up when adult says, "Carry you?"	Says, "More milk" or "No naptime" or "You read this." Pretends a block is a cracker and pretends to eat it. Hits or bites to communicate with another child.	Follows directions when told "Wash your hands, then find a seat at the cooking table." Says, "I want to paint" or "My dog ranned away and he didn't come back and my brother he tried to find it."	Follows directions when told "Come get your body traced, then paint your face on it, and write your name on the page." Says, "My brother cried because the dog got lost." Talks with others at the snack table about a movie they all saw.

	Infant	Young Toddler	Older Toddler	Preschooler	Pre-kindergartener
Recognizes that she can do things, make things happen, and solve problems (self-efficacy)	Tries communicating with others through noises and body language. Explores by doing the same thing over and over again.	Figures out how to solve problems without considering the effect on others. Seeks adult help to solve problems.	Seeks adult attention to get positive feedback or help. Insists on doing things by himself. Explores physical cause and effect.	Asserts needs and wants without hurting or violating others. Completes multistep tasks without adult help. Uses learned social skills for sharing space and stuff.	Attempts several ways to do something complex if one way doesn't work. Begins to create original solutions to problems.
Examples	Lets others know that he wants to be picked up or played with. Turns head away when done feeding. Kicks at a mobile hung overhead.	Bangs an empty bowl on the table to get more cereal. Sits on another child to be closer to a book. Drops a shoe on the adult's lap to get help putting it on.	Calls, "Look" when climbs steps up the slide. Pushes adult hand away when trying to zip jacket. Shouts, "Me do it," when adult tries to help. Flushes toilet over and over to see what happens. Turns water on in sink and holds hand over the drain to see what happens.	Says, "My turn" to a child on the swing. Cuts out pictures and glues them onto the pages of a self-made book. Takes turns throwing the ball in the basket.	Tries a number of ways to tape two boxes together to make a dog house. Says, "I know! How about we make some more cars out of the Legos?"

	Infant	Young Toddler	Older Toddler	Preschooler	Pre-kindergartener
Develops an understanding of self and relationship to others	Reacts to facial expressions. Communicates needs through body language, crying.	Recognizes self and familiar people. Changes behavior in reaction to another's emotions.	Differentiates self from caregivers—demonstrates ambivalence of wanting to be connected and separate. Expresses ideas about self and connection to others. Is aware of and reacts to others' feelings.	Follows adult guidance about sharing space and stuff. Responds to peer assertion of needs or wants.	Uses words or actions to respond with caring to others' emotions. Can predict how another might react in a given situation. Tries to make amends when has wronged another.
Examples	Smiles and coos in response to others. Cries when hungry or tired.	Recognizes self in mirror. Points to photo of grandma and says, "Nana." Laughs and claps when another child laughs and claps.	Says, "No" and runs away when called. Then runs back weeping and asking to be picked up. Runs to hug older brother in the preschool room, calling him by name. Sees child crying and goes to adult saying, "Reena crying."	With adult prompting, moves over at circle time to let another child sit down. With adult reminder, passes the bowl of potatoes to next child at lunch. Lets another child join in at home living center when child asks, "Can I play with you?"	Says, "Let me see your owie. Does it hurt?" When provider asks about how the little pig might feel when the wolf is chasing him, says, "He gets scared." Says, "Sorry," when accidentally steps on another child's hand. .

APPENDIX B
Common Social/Emotional Screening Tools for Young Children

Acronym	Name	Used for assessing	Ages
	The Ounce Scale	social interactions, feelings about self, communication, problem solving, physical coordination	infant, toddler
ASQ-SE	Ages and Stages Questionnaires: Social Emotional	self-regulation, compliance, communication, adaptive functioning, autonomy, affect, interactions with people	6–, 12–, 18–, 24–, 30–, 36–, 48– and 60–month versions
BASC-2	Behavior Assessment System for Children	adaptability, aggression, anxiety, attention, atypicality, conduct, depression, functional communication, hyperactivity, social skills, somatization, withdrawal	2–5 years
BSID-III	Bayley Scales of Infant and Toddler Development, Third Edition	cognitive, language, motor, adaptive, social/emotional behavior	1 month–42 months
CARS	Childhood Autism Rating Scale	autism	2+ years
CBCL	Child Behavior Checklist	child behavior and social competency as reported by parents	1–5 years

Acronym	Name	Used for assessing	Ages
CRS-R	Conners Rating Scale	ADHD	3–5 years
DECA	Devereaux Early Childhood Assessment	self-regulation, initiative, and attachment	2–5 years
ECBI	Eyberg Child Behavior Inventory	conduct disorders	2–16 years
FEAS	Functional Emotional Assessment Scale	emotional functioning	birth–42 months
NBAS	Neonatal Behavioral Assessment Scale	responsiveness, soothability, and adaptability of newborn	birth–2 months
PKBS-2	Preschool and Kindergarten Behavior Scales	social skills, problem solving	3–6 years
TABS	Temperament and Atypical Behavior Scale	temperament and self-regulation	11–71 months
Vineland II	Vineland Adaptive Behavior Scales, Second Edition	social development and problem behaviors, communication, motor-development skills, daily living skills	3+ years

APPENDIX C
Common Medications Prescribed for Children to Reduce Psychiatric Symptoms

The following information is intended to supplement, not substitute for, the expertise and judgment of the child's physician, pharmacist, or other health care professional. These medications may be prescribed as part of a comprehensive treatment plan that may also include therapy, changes to environment, and adult-child interactions.

Additional information may be needed from caregivers in order to determine what medication is being given, why it is being given, and what side effects you might see in the child.

Brand name	Generic name	Class of medication	Most common uses	Possible side effects
Adderall	Amphetamine	Stimulant	ADHD	Irritability, increase in excitability or impulsivity, loss of appetite, trouble sleeping, tics
Adderall XR	Amphetamine	Stimulant	ADHD	Irritability, increase in excitability or impulsivity, loss of appetite, trouble sleeping, tics
Catapres	Clonidine	Antihypertensive	ADHD with Tourette's,* PTSD	Headache, stomach-ache, drowsiness, dizziness, nausea, depression
Concerta	Methylphenidate	Stimulant	ADHD	Headache, stomachache, loss of appetite, trouble sleeping, dizziness, nausea, irritability
Cylert	Pemoline	Stimulant	ADHD	Irritability, increase in excitability or impulsivity, loss of appetite, trouble sleeping, tics, liver disease

* Tourette's syndrome is a rare disorder characterized by involuntary physical and vocal tics, including eye blinks, grimaces, grunts, and inappropriate words. Tourette's is not covered in this book.

Brand name	Generic name	Class of medication	Most common uses	Possible side effects
Depakote	Valproic Acid	Anticonvulsant	Seizures, bipolar disorder	Nausea, increased appetite, weight gain, drowsiness, tremors
Dexedrine	Dextroampheta-mine	Stimulant	ADHD	Irritability, increase in excitability or impulsivity, loss of appetite, trouble sleeping, tics
Dextrostat	Dextroampheta-mine	Stimulant	ADHD	Nausea, stomach-ache, loss of appetite, dry mouth, headache, nervousness, dizzi-ness, sleep prob-lems, irritability, restlessness, twitching, tremors
Focalin	Dexmethylphen-idate	Stimulant	ADHD	Trouble sleeping, nausea, diarrhea, upset stomach, dizziness, headache, nerv-ousness, loss of appetite, dry mouth, weight loss
Lithobid, Lithonate, Lithotabs, Cibalith, Eskalith	Lithium carbonate	Mood stabilizer	Bipolar disorder	Nausea, sleepi-ness, thirst, increased urina-tion, weight gain, tremors, changes in thyroid or kid-ney function
Luvox	Fluvoxamine	Antidepressant	OCD, anxiety	Headache, dizzi-ness, nausea, trouble sleeping, anxiety
Mellaril	Thiothixene	Antipsychotic	Psychosis, autism, PDD, Tourette's*	Sleepiness, diffi-culty learning, weight gain, rest-lessness, abnormal motor movements

* Tourette's syndrome is a rare disorder characterized by involuntary physical and vocal tics, including eye blinks, grimaces, grunts, and inappropriate words. Tourette's is not covered in this book.

Brand name	Generic name	Class of medication	Most common uses	Possible side effects
Metadate ER	Methylphenidate	Stimulant	ADHD	Headache, stomachache, loss of appetite, trouble sleeping, dizziness, nausea, lightheadedness, irritability, nervousness, dry mouth
Paxil	Paroxetine	Antidepressant	Depression, anxiety	Headache, dizziness, nausea, trouble sleeping, anxiety
Prozac	Fluoxetine	Antidepressant	Depression, PTSD, OCD, anxiety	Headache, dizziness, nausea, trouble sleeping, anxiety, suicidal thoughts
Risperdal	Risperidone	Antipsychotic	Schizophrenia	Weight gain, drowsiness, dizziness, nausea
Ritalin	Methylphenidate	Stimulant	ADHD	Irritability, increase in excitability or impulsivity, loss of appetite, trouble sleeping, tics
Seroquel	Quetiapine	Antipsychotic	Schizophrenia	Sleepiness, dizziness, flu-like symptoms, loss of appetite
Strattera	Atomoxetine	Nonstimulant	ADHD, Tourette's*	Loss of appetite, weight loss, stomachache, nausea, fatigue, dry mouth, dizziness, trouble sleeping, mood changes

* Tourette's syndrome is a rare disorder characterized by involuntary physical and vocal tics, including eye blinks, grimaces, grunts, and inappropriate words. Tourette's is not covered in this book.

Brand name	Generic name	Class of medication	Most common uses	Possible side effects
Tegretol	Carbamazepine	Anticonvulsant	Seizures, bipolar disorder, ADHD	Headache, stomachache
Tenex	Guanfacine	Antihypertensive	ADHD	Headache, dizziness, nausea, trouble sleeping, anxiety
Thorazine	Chlorpromazine	Antipsychotic	Psychosis, autism, PDD, Tourette's	Sleepiness, difficulty learning, weight gain, restlessness, abnormal motor movements
Tofranil	Imipramine	Antidepressant	Bedwetting, ADHD	Rapid heartbeat, dry mouth, rash
Wellbutrin	Buproprion	Antidepressant	ADHD with depression	Tiredness, nausea, loss of appetite, dizziness, headache, tremors
Zoloft	Sertraline	Antidepressant	Depression, OCD, anxiety	Headache, dizziness, nausea, trouble sleeping, anxiety
Zyprexa	Olanzapine	Antipsychotic	Schizophrenia, bipolar disorder	Dizziness, drowsiness, weight gain

* Tourette's syndrome is a rare disorder characterized by involuntary physical and vocal tics, including eye blinks, grimaces, grunts, and inappropriate words. Tourette's is not covered in this book.

APPENDIX D
Additional Resources for Families and Early Childhood Professionals

ONLINE RESOURCES

About Our Kids

http://www.aboutourkids.org

The New York University Child Study Center is dedicated to increasing the awareness of child mental health issues and improving the treatment of child psychiatric illnesses through scientific practice, research, and education.

Information also available in Spanish. Some resources available in Korean and Chinese.

ADD Resources

http://www.addresources.org

Founded in 1993, Attention Deficit Disorder Resources (ADD Resources) is a nonprofit organization run mostly by adult volunteers with ADHD dedicated to supporting, educating, and serving as a resource for people with ADHD. ADD Resources maintains an educational Web site, a bookstore, and a lending library with over 450 titles of ADHD books, audiotapes, and videos. They publish a monthly eNews, the 8-page ADDult ADDvice quarterly newsletter, the 138-page Adult ADD Reader, and an outstanding collection of articles by national ADHD authorities as well as adults with ADHD.

American Academy of Child and Adolescent Psychiatry

http://www.aacap.org

Established in 1953, the American Academy of Child and Adolescent Psychiatry is a professional medical organization composed of child and adolescent psychiatrists trained to promote healthy development and to evaluate, diagnose, and treat children and adolescents and their families who are affected by disorders of feeling, thinking, and behavior. Information is provided as a public service to aid in the understanding and treatment of developmental, behavioral, and mental disorders. You will find fact sheets for parents and caregivers plus information on child and adolescent psychiatry, AACAP membership, current research, practice guidelines, managed care, awards and fellowships, meetings, and more.

This Web site is also available in Spanish.

"Facts for Families" pages are available in English, Spanish, German, French, Malaysian, Polish, and Icelandic.

Anxiety Disorders Association of America

http://www.adaa.org

http://www.adaa.org/GettingHelp/FocusOn/Children&Adolescents.asp (information specific to children)

Established in 1980, the Anxiety Disorders Association of America (ADAA) is a nonprofit organization whose mission is to promote the prevention, treatment, and cure of anxiety disorders and to improve the lives of all people who suffer from them.

Autism Society of America (ASA)

http://www.autism-society.org

Founded in 1965, ASA encompasses a broad, diverse group of parents, family members, special education teachers, administrators, medical doctors, therapists, nurses, and aides, as well as those involved in the education, care, treatment, and support of individuals with autism. Recognizing and respecting the diverse range of opinions, needs, and desires of this group, ASA embraces an overall philosophy that chooses to empower individuals with autism and their parents or caregivers to make choices best suited to the needs of the person with autism.

Information is also available in Spanish.

Bright Futures: Guidelines for Health Supervision of Infants, Children, and Adolescents

http://brightfutures.aap.org

Bright Futures, which was initiated by the Maternal and Child Health Bureau (MCHB) over a decade ago, is a philosophy and approach that is dedicated to the principle that every child deserves to be healthy and that optimal health involves a trusting relationship between the health professional, the child, the family, and the community. Use the link http://brightfutures.aap.org/web/FamiliesandCommunitiestoolsAndResources.asp to access the two-part online version of Bright Futures in Practice: Mental Health.

CHADD: Children and Adults with Attention-Deficit/ Hyperactivity Disorder

http://www.chadd.org

Founded in 1987, CHADD works to improve the lives of people affected by ADHD through collaborative leadership, advocacy, research, education, and support. CHADD has over 16,000 members in 200 local chapters throughout the United States. Chapters offer support for individuals, parents, teachers, professionals, and others.

Information on this site is also available in Spanish.

Child Advocate

http://www.childadvocate.net/childmentalhealth

Information at this link addresses mental disorders, behavioral disorders, child abuse, trauma, disaster, and advocacy issues. The link also provides information including child mental health news and research results.

Child and Adolescent Bipolar Foundation

http://www.bpkids.org

The Child and Adolescent Bipolar Foundation educates families, professionals, and the public about pediatric bipolar disorder; connects families with resources and support; advocates for and empowers affected families; and supports research on pediatric bipolar disorder and its cure.

Child and Family WebGuide

http://www.cfw.tufts.edu

This Web resource links to and rates Web sites on topics of interest to parents and professionals. All the sites listed on the WebGuide have been evaluated by graduate students and faculty in child development. The goal of the WebGuide is to give the public easy access to the best child development information on the Web.

Kids Health

http://kidshealth.org

http://kidshealth.org/parent/emotions/index.html (for behavior and mental health information for families)

Created by the Nemours Foundation's Center for Children's Health Media, KidsHealth provides families with up-to-date and parent-friendly health information.

Maternal and Child Health Library

http://www.mchlibrary.info
The MCH Library is part of the National Center for Education in Maternal and Child Health (NCEMCH) at Georgetown University. Founded in 1982, NCEMCH provides leadership and state-of-the-art knowledge related to MCH issues to help federal, state, and local policymakers, public health professionals, and the public make informed decisions about MCH services, programs, and policies.

Use the A-Z link, and then select Child Mental Health—Knowledge Path. This will guide you to a wide variety of resources.

NARSAD: The Mental Health Research Association

http://www.narsad.org
Originally incorporated in 1981 as the American Schizophrenia Foundation, NARSAD is now a powerful alliance of the three leading national mental health and illness organizations: the National Alliance for the Mentally Ill, the National Mental Health Association, and the National Depressive and Manic Depressive Association.

Although there is no special "kid" section on this site, by typing "children" into the search box, you'll be directed to many valuable resources.

National Institute of Mental Health

http://www.nimh.nih.gov
http://www.nimh.nih.gov/healthinformation/childmenu.cfm
(information specific to children)
The National Institute of Mental Health (NIMH) is one of twenty-seven components of the National Institutes of Health (NIH), the federal government's principal biomedical and behavioral research agency. NIH is part of the U.S. Department of Health and Human Services.

Some family information is available in Spanish.

National Mental Health Association

http://www.nmha.org
http://www.nmha.org/infoctr/factsheets/index.cfm#children
(information specific to children)
Established in 1909, the National Mental Health Association (NMHA) is the country's oldest and largest nonprofit organization addressing all aspects of mental health and mental illness. With more than 340 affiliates nationwide,

NMHA works to improve the mental health of all Americans, especially the 54 million individuals with mental disorders, through advocacy, education, research, and service.

National Mental Health Information Center, Center for Mental Health Services. U.S. Department of Health and Human Services, Substance Abuse and Mental Health Services Administration (SAMHSA)

http://www.mentalhealth.samhsa.gov
http://www.mentalhealth.samhsa.gov/child/childhealth.asp
(info specific to children)
Systems of care are developed on the premise that the mental health needs of children, adolescents, and their families can be met within their home, school, and community environments. These systems are developed around these principles: child-centered, family-driven, strength-based, and culturally competent, with interagency collaboration. The Child, Adolescent, and Family Branch embraces and promotes these core principles of systems of care.

Limited parent resources in Spanish.

Radkid.org: Reactive Attachment Disorder

http://www.radkid.org
RadKid.org seeks to serve as a resource and source of mutual support for parents or others who are parenting children with reactive attachment disorder. This site, and its companion group at http://forums.delphiforums.com/radkid/ are intended to support, not replace, the relationship that should exist between a site visitor and his or her child's physician or therapist. The persons responsible for maintaining RadKid.org are persons parenting a child with reactive attachment disorder, not mental health professionals.

Zero to Three

http://www.zerotothree.org
Established in 1977, Zero to Three's mission is to support the healthy development and well-being of infants, toddlers, and their families. This national, nonprofit, multidisciplinary organization advances its mission by informing, educating, and supporting adults who influence the lives of children from birth to age three. This Web site has information for both parents and early childhood professionals.

Some resources available in Spanish.

PRINT RESOURCES

The Autism Book: Answers to Your Most Pressing Questions. Jhoanna Robledo and Dawn Ham-Kucharski. New York: Penguin Books, 2005.
S. Jhoanna Robledo, a graduate of the Columbia School of Journalism, is a freelance writer specializing in parenting and health. Dawn Ham-Kucharski is on the board of directors of the Michigan Autism Partnership and serves as the outreach coordinator for the PLAY Project.

The Bipolar Child: The Definitive and Reassuring Guide to Childhood's Most Misunderstood Disorder. Revised and expanded edition, Demitri Papolos, MD, and Janice Papolos. New York: Broadway Books. 2002.
Dr. Papolos is an associate professor of psychiatry at the Albert Einstein College of Medicine and the codirector of the Program in Behavioral Genetics. He is the director of research for the Juvenile Bipolar Research Foundation.

Children and Trauma: A Guide for Parents and Professionals. Cynthia Monahon. San Francisco: Jossey-Bass, 1997.
Cynthia Monahon is director of a children's mental health clinic in Massachusetts.

The Difficult Child. Second revised edition. Stanley Turecki, MD. New York: Bantam Books, 2000.
Dr. Turecki is a child and family psychiatrist and a diplomate of the American Board of Psychiatry and Neurology.

Easy to Love, Difficult to Discipline: The 7 Basic Skills for Turning Conflict into Cooperation. Becky Bailey, PhD. New York: HarperCollins, 2002.
Dr. Bailey is a former associate professor of early childhood education at the University of Central Florida. She is president of Living Guidance, Inc.

The Everything Parent's Guide to Children with Autism: Know What to Expect, Find the Help You Need, and Get Through the Day. Adelle Jameson Tilton. Avon, MA: Adams Media, 2004.
Adelle Jameson Tilton is the autism guide on About.com and the mother of a son with autism. She is a member of the Autism Society of America and has served as secretary for WAYSAC, a Michigan autism organization.

The Explosive Child: A New Approach for Understanding and Parenting Easily Frustrated "Chronically Inflexible" Children. Second edition. Ross W. Greene, PhD. New York: Harper Paperbacks, 2001.
Dr. Greene is the director of the Problem Solving Institute in the Department of Psychiatry at Massachusetts General Hospital.

The Heart of Parenting: Raising an Emotionally Intelligent Child. John Gottman, PhD, with Joan DeClaire. New York: Fireside, 1997.
Dr. Gottman is professor of psychology at the University of Washington. Joan DeClaire is senior editor for an online consumer health information service.

How to Talk So Kids Will Listen and Listen So Kids Will Talk. Adele Faber and Elaine Mazlish. New York: HarperCollins, 1980.
Both authors studied with child psychologist Dr. Ginott. Their books are best sellers, and they run numerous parent workshops and produce videos with PBS.

The Irreducible Needs of Children: What Every Child Must Have to Grow, Learn, and Flourish. T. Berry Brazelton, MD, and Stanley I. Greenspan, MD. Cambridge, MA: Perseus Publishing, 2001.
Dr. Brazelton is professor emeritus of pediatrics at Harvard Medical School and founder of the Child Development Unit at Children's Hospital in Boston. Dr. Greenspan is clinical professor of psychiatry and pediatrics at George Washington University School of Medicine and founding president of Zero to Three.

The OASIS Guide to Asperger Syndrome: Completely Revised and Updated: Advice, Support, Insight, and Inspiration. Patricia Romanowski Bashe and Barbara L. Kirby. New York: Crown Publishers, 2005.
Bashe is a special education teacher and executive director of the nonprofit David Center for children with autism. Kirby moderates a number of online forums addressing autism. Both authors have children with Asperger's.

The Out-of-Sync Child: Recognizing and Coping with Sensory Integration Dysfunction. Carol Stock Kranowitz. New York: Skylight Press, 1998. Also, *The Out-Of Sync Child Has Fun: Activities for Kids with Sensory Integration Dysfunction.* Carol Stock Kranowitz. New York: Perigee, 2003.
Kranowitz has taught preschool for twenty-five years, specializing in children with sensory integration dysfunction.

Parenting from the Inside Out: How a Deeper Self-Understanding Can Help You Raise Children Who Thrive. Daniel J. Siegel, MD, and Mary Hartzell. New York: Tarcher/Putnam, 2003.
Dr. Siegel, a graduate of Harvard University, is associate clinical professor of psychiatry at the Center for Culture, Brain and Development at UCLA. Mary Hartzell has a master's degree in early childhood and is a child development specialist and parent educator.

Raising a Moody Child: How to Cope with Depression and Bipolar Disorder. Mary A. Fristad, PhD, and Jill S. Goldberg Arnold, PhD. New York: Guilford Press, 2004.
Dr. Fristad is professor of psychiatry and psychology at Ohio State University and director of research and psychological services in the OSU Division of Child and Adolescent Psychiatry. Dr. Arnold is clinical assistant professor of psychiatry at Ohio State University. She is now in private practice.

Straight Talk about Psychiatric Medications for Kids. Revised edition. Timothy E. Wilens, MD. New York: Guilford Press, 2004.
Dr. Wilens is associate professor of psychiatry at Harvard Medical School. He is a specialist in pediatric and adult psychopharmacology at Massachusetts General Hospital.

Straight Talk about Psychological Testing for Kids. Ellen Braaten and Gretchen Felopulos. New York: Guilford Press, 2003.
Braaten and Felopulos are staff psychologists at the Psychology Assessment Center at Massachusetts General Hospital for Children and are on the faculty at Harvard Medical School's Department of Psychiatry.

Touchpoints: Both Volumes of the Nation's Most Trusted Guide to the First Six Years of Life. T. Berry Brazelton, MD. New York: Perseus Books Group, 2002.
Dr. Brazelton is professor emeritus of pediatrics at Harvard Medical School and founder of the Child Development Unit at Children's Hospital in Boston.

The Worried Child: Recognizing Anxiety in Children and Helping Them Heal. Paul Foxman, PhD. Alameda, CA: Hunter House, 2004.
Dr. Foxman is a psychologist and the director of the Center for Anxiety Disorders in Vermont.

BIBLIOGRAPHY

American Academy of Child and Adolescent Psychiatry. 2004. Psychiatric medication for children and adolescents. Part II: types of medications. Facts for Families Information Sheet No. 29. http://www.aacap.org.

American Academy of Child and Adolescent Psychiatry. 2005. Practice parameters for the assessment and treatment of children and adolescents with reactive attachment disorder of infancy and early childhood. http://www.aacap.org/clinical/parameters/fulltext/rad.pdf.

American Psychiatric Association. 2006. Children, mental illness and medicines. http://www.healthyminds.org.

American Psychiatric Association. 2000. DSM-IV-TR: *Diagnostic and statistical manual of mental disorders.* 4th ed. Text Revision. Washington, DC: American Psychiatric Association Press.

Bailey, R. A. 2001. *Conscious discipline.* Lewisville, NC: Kaplan Early Learning Company.

Bates, J. E., et al. 1991. Origins of externalizing behavior problems at eight years of age. In D. J. Pepler and K. H. Rubin, eds., *The development and treatment of childhood aggression*, 93–120. Hillsdale, NJ: Erlbaum.

Beebe, B., and F. M. Lachmann. 2002. *Infant research and adult treatment.* Hillsdale, NJ: The Analytic Press, Inc.

Bilmes, J. 2004. *Beyond behavior management: The six life skills children need to thrive in today's world.* St. Paul, MN: Redleaf Press.

Campbell, S. B. 1995. Behavior problems in preschool children: A review of recent research. *Journal of Child Psychology and Psychiatry* 36: 113–49.

Clark, A., and S. Lewis. 1998. Practitioner review: Treatment of schizophrenia in childhood and adolescence. *Journal of Child Psychology and Psychiatry* 39 (8): 1071–81.

Copple, C., ed. 2003. *A world of difference: Readings on teaching young children in a diverse society.* Washington, DC: NAEYC.

Crockenberg, S., and E. Leerkes. 2000. Infant social and emotional development in family context. In *Handbook of Infant Mental Health*, edited by C. H. Zeanah, 60–90. 2nd ed. New York: Guilford Press.

DeGangi, G. 2000. *Pediatric disorders of regulation in affect and behavior: A therapist's guide to assessment and treatment.* San Diego: Academic Press.

Dulmus, C. N., and Smyth, N. J. 2000. Early-onset schizophrenia: A literature review of empirically based interventions. *Child and Adolescent Social Work Journal* 17: 55–69.

Finello, K. M., ed. 2005. *The handbook of training and practice in infant and preschool mental health.* San Francisco: Jossey-Bass.

Fraser, K. M. 2002. Too young for attention deficit disorder? Views from preschool. *Journal of Developmental and Behavioral Pediatrics* 23 (Sup. 1): S46–S50.

Gimpel, G. A., and M. L. Holland. 2003. *Emotional and behavioral problems of young children: Effective interventions in the preschool and kindergarten years.* New York: The Guilford Press.

Gomi, Taro. 1993. *Everyone poops.* La Jolla, CA: Kane/Miller.

Gonthier, M., and M. A. Lyon. 2004. Childhood onset schizophrenia: An overview. *Psychology in the Schools* 41 (7): 803–11.

Gorman-Smith, D. 2003. Effects of teacher training and consultation on teacher behavior toward students at high risk for aggression. *Behavior Therapy* 34: 437–52.

Greenspan, S. I. 2006. *Engaging autism: Helping children relate, communicate and think with the DIR floortime approach.* New York: Perseus Books Group.

———. 1997. *Developmentally based psychotherapy.* Madison, CT: International Universities Press.

Greenspan, S. I., S. Wieder, PhD, and R. Simons. 1998. *The child with special needs: Encouraging intellectual and emotional growth.* Cambridge, MA: Perseus Publishing.

Gutstein, S. E. 2001. *Autism Asperger's: Solving the relationship puzzle—a new developmental program that opens the door to lifelong social and emotional growth.* Arlington, TX: Future Horizons.

Hoagwood, K., et al. 1996. Outcomes of mental health care for children and adolescents: I. A comprehensive conceptual model. *Journal of the American Academy of Child and Adolescent Psychiatry* 35: 1055–63.

Holzwarth, Werner, and W. Erlbruch. 1993. *The story of the little mole who went in search of whodunit.* New York: Stewart, Tabori, and Chang.

Kaiser, B., and J. S. Rasminsky. 2003. *Challenging behavior in young children: Understanding, preventing and responding effectively.* Boston: Allyn and Bacon.

Kessler, R. C., et al. 2005. Prevalence, severity, and comorbidity of twelve-month DSM-IV disorders in the National Comorbidity Survey Replication (NCS-R). *Archives of General Psychiatry* 62 (6): 617–27.

Koplow, L. 2002. *Creating schools that heal: Real-life solutions.* New York: Teachers College Press.

Koralek, D. 1999. *For now and forever: A guide for families on promoting social and emotional development.* Villanova, PA: The Devereux Foundation.

Kranowitz, C. S. 1998. *The out-of-sync child: Recognizing and coping with sensory integration dysfunction.* New York: Skylight Press.

Kremer, D., and J. David, eds. 2002. *Head Start bulletin: Child mental health*, Issue 73. Washington, DC: Head Start Bureau.

Linder, T. W. 1993. *Transdisciplinary play-based assessment: A functional approach to working with young children.* Baltimore: Paul H. Brooks Publishing.

Linfoot, K., A. J. Martin, and J. Stephenson. 1999. Preventing conduct disorder: A study of parental behaviour management and support needs in children aged 3 to 5 years. *International Journal of Disability, Development and Education* 46 (2): 223–46.

Lynch, E. W., and M. J. Hanson. 1998. *Developing cross-cultural competence: A guide to working with children and their families.* Second edition. Baltimore: Paul H. Brookes Publishing.

Mann, T. 1998. Promoting mental health of infants and toddlers in Early Head Start: Responsibilities, partnerships and supports. *Zero to Three* 18 (2): 37–40.

Marshall, H. H. 2001. Cultural influences on the development of self-concept: Updating our thinking. *Young Children* 56 (6): 19–22.

Marvin, R. S., and P. A. Britner. 1999. Normative development: The ontogeny of attachment. In *Handbook of Attachment*, edited by J. Cassidy and P. R. Shaver, 44–67. New York: Guilford Press.

Mick, E., et al. 2003. Defining a developmental subtype of bipolar disorder in a sample of non-referred adults by age at onset. *Journal of Child and Adolescent Psychopharmacology* 13: 453–62.

Minnesota Association for Children's Mental Health. 2005. *A teacher's guide to children's mental health.* St. Paul, MN: MACMH.

Munsch, Robert. 1987. *I have to go!* Toronto, ONT, Canada: Annick Press.

National Institute of Mental Health. 2002. *Medications.* Bethesda, MD: National Institute of Mental Health, National Institutes of Health, U.S. Department of Health and Human Services.

National Research Council and Institute of Medicine. 2000. *From neurons to neighborhoods: The science of early childhood development.* Washington, DC: National Academy Press.

Papolos, D., and J. Papolos. 2002. *The bipolar child: The definitive and reassuring guide to childhood's most misunderstood disorder.* New York: Broadway Books.

Parlakian, R., and N. L. Seibel. 2002. *Building strong foundations: Practical guidance for promoting the social-emotional development of infants and toddlers.* Washington, DC: Zero to Three.

Perry, B. D., et al. 1995. Childhood trauma, the neurobiology of adaptation, and "use-dependent" development of the brain: How "states" become "traits." *Infant Mental Health Journal* 16 (4): 271–91.

Quinn, M. M., et al. 2000. *Teaching and working with children who have emotional and behavioral challenges.* Longmont, CO: Sopris West.

Rimm-Kaufman, S. E., R. C. Pianta, and M. J. Cox. 2000. Teacher's judgments of problems in the transition to kindergarten. *Early Childhood Research Quarterly* 15: 147–66.

Scheeringa, M. S., and T. J. Gaensbauer. 2000. Posttraumatic stress disorder. In *Handbook of Infant Mental Health*, edited by C. H. Zeanah Jr., 369–81. 2nd ed. New York: Guilford Press.

Scheeringa, M. S., and C. H. Zeanah. 1995. Symptom expression and trauma variables in children under 48 months of age. *Infant Mental Health Journal* 16 (4): 259–70.

Schore, A. N. 1999. *Affect regulation and the origin of the self: The neurobiology of emotional development*. Mahwah, NJ: Lawrence Erlbaum Associates.

Schore, A. N. 2001. The effects of early relational trauma on the right brain development, affect regulation, and infant mental health. *Infant Mental Health Journal* 22 (1–2): 201–69.

Shore, R. 1997. *Rethinking the brain: New insights into early development*. New York: Families and Work Institute.

Spitz, R. 1946. Hospitalism: A follow-up report. *Psychoanalytic Study of the Child* 2: 313–42.

Surgeon General, U.S. Public Health Service. 1999. *Mental health: A report of the surgeon general*. Washington, DC: Government Printing Office.

Thomas, A., and S. Chess. 1977. *Temperament and development*. New York: Brunner/Mazel.

U.S. Department of Health and Human Services. 1999. *Mental health: A report of the surgeon general—Executive summary*. Rockville, MD: U.S. Department of Health and Human Services, Substance Abuse and Mental Health Services Administration, Center for Mental Health Services, National Institutes of Health, National Institute of Mental Health.

Webster-Stratton, C. 1993. Strategies for helping early school-aged children with oppositional defiant and conduct disorders: The importance of home-school partnerships. *School Psychology Review* 22 (3): 437–57.

Webster-Stratton, C., M. J. Reid, and M. Hammond. 2001. Preventing conduct problems, promoting social competence: A parent and teacher training partnership in Head Start. *Journal of Clinical Child Psychology* 30 (3): 283–302.

———. 2004. Treating children with early-onset conduct problems: Intervention outcomes for parent, child, and teacher training. *Journal of Clinical Child and Adolescent Psychology* 33 (1): 105–24.

Weyandt, L. L. 2005. Executive function in children, adolescents, and adults with attention deficit hyperactivity disorder: Introduction to the special issue. *Developmental Neuropsychology* 27 (1): 1–10.

Wilens, T. E. 2004. *Straight talk about psychiatric medications for kids*. New York: Guilford Press.

Yoshikawa, H., and J. Knitzer. 1996. *Lessons from the field: Head Start mental health strategies to meet challenging needs*. New York: National Center for Children in Poverty.

Zero to Three. 1992. *The zero to three child care anthology 1984–1992*. Arlington, VA: National Center for Clinical Infant Programs.

Zero to Three. 2005. DC:0–3R: *Diagnostic classification of mental health and developmental disorders of infancy and early childhood*. Revised edition. Washington, DC: Zero to Three Press.

FINAL THOUGHTS

The important thing is not to stop questioning. Curiosity has its own reason for existing. One cannot help but be in awe when he contemplates the mysteries of eternity, of life, of the marvelous structure of reality. It is enough if one tries merely to comprehend a little of this mystery every day. —ALBERT EINSTEIN

ABOUT THE AUTHORS

Jenna Bilmes is a mental health specialist with FACES of Crisis Nursery in Phoenix and a consultant for the U.S. Department of Defense Dependent Schools and Sonoma State University. She is the author of *Beyond Behavior Management* (Redleaf Press, 2004). To learn more about Jenna and her work, please visit her Web site at www.kidsfromtheinsideout.com.

Tara Welker, PhD, is a licensed psychologist in private practice in Phoenix. She has done clinical research at the New York State Psychiatric Institute and has spent over two years providing treatment and assessment services to young children at Southwest Human Development.

INDEX

Other Resources from Redleaf Press